'Sophie Fox's book, 'Guided by ⬛⬛⬛ gel
lover's collection. It's informat eel
privileged to be 'invited along f. nal
angel journey, then make full use of her tips and tricks, to enhance
your own angelic experience. Everyone should own this book!

Jacky Newcomb, Sunday Times bestselling author of 'An Angel Saved My Life' and 'An Angel by my Side'.

'I do love Sophie's book 'Guided by Angels.' It is exactly what we
need in times of change and uncertainty. It is beautifully written,
easy to work with and packed with information that will raise your
vibration and make your soul sing. Whatever you are looking for,
'Guided by Angels' will have something very special for you.'

Anne Jirsch, bestselling author, international trainer.

'Guided by Angels' is not just a book about angels, it is filled with
heart-felt and very practical advice for all stages of life. Whether you
are at the beginning and just awakening to the call of your soul, or
already work alongside the angelic realms, you will find inspiration
and wisdom here. Lots of hard work goes into every book and this
is certainly the case for Sophie Fox who has invested love and
experience woven into her guidance. The loving warmth is tangible.'

Chrissie Astell, one of the UK's best-loved spiritual educators and angel experts.

GUIDED BY ANGELS

A JOURNEY THROUGH
LIFE WITH THE ARCHANGELS

by Sophie Fox

ISBN: 978-1-9162504-5-1

As a special thank you for purchasing this book, please find 10 audio meditations available here:-

www.angelicenergies.co.uk/guided-meditations

Password: Angels

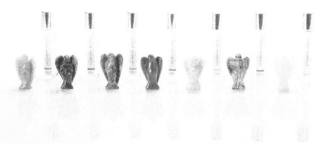

RELEASE ALL DOUBT,
FEAR AND UNCERTAINTY
AND GAIN A CLEAR
VISION OF YOUR
PERFECT FUTURE BY

FUTURE
LIFE
PROGRESSION

WITH SOPHIE FOX AT
ANGELIC ENERGIES

FIND OUT MORE AT
WWW.ANGELICENERGIES.CO.UK

This book is dedicated to my children, Otto and Aluna. I wish I had known this information while I was growing up, and it is my hope that they will have a stronger future as a result.

with love

&

Angel blessings

Sophie

X

Acknowledgements

I am eternally grateful to the enigmatic and gifted Stewart Pearce, international bestselling author of 'Angels of Atlantis', 'The Alchemy of Voice' and 'Diana, The Voice for Change' to name but a few. He generously give his time and consideration to adjust the finer points of this body of work, enabling it to become its full intended expression in accordance with the Angels. He is truly a brilliant, incredibly compassionate and enlightened Earth Angel of our time and his work to empower people through the power of their voice is truly transformational.

I would like to extend a special thanks to Jan Costello, healer and communicator with higher energies, for giving me the strength and the confirmation needed to get this book finished. Words cannot express my gratitude. Thanks also to Claire Louise Webster at A Colourful You for giving a voice to the Angels and team of spiritual support. Thank you to Maria Lau Binks and her creative technical genius, to my brother Peter Carter with Centauri Perfumes and Fragrance View, to my mother Lorna for her amazing support, and my husband Chris for always believing in me and offering the best advice. Last but not least, thank you to my wonderful guides in spirit for continually pushing me to get this book out into the world.

FOREWORD BY STEWART PEARCE

Angels generate beams of light that laser through the dark bringing thoughts from the mind of the God directly to our bidding. Sophie's writing reveals such light, for through her truthful thought records and practical work, it is via such earthly terms that the Angels show their faces. On occasions in life one meets a gem-person who glimmers with light, knowing, humility, grace and love. When we meet one can feel them to be charged with a heavenly task, and this I feel is the way for Sophie.

I write these thoughts in July 2020, and it's not difficult to reflect on the fact that a heavy-weight Global era is in its final stages of completion. Around the world we can see vast change, brought about by the societal shifts of Covid 19, economic uncertainty, urban unrest, corporate chicanery and the shifting sub-strata of our Central Governments. It's apparent that all our Governing systems need re-evaluating and re-defining, and as anxiety precedes change the quaking surface of our world can also make us feel frightened, isolated and lonely - until that is we kneel in prayer, in meditation or in loving chant. Then we feel the Angels meet our hearts, our energy fields, our intuition, and our soul's compass - for this is their favor and divine charge!

"To see an Angel, we must see another's Soul,

To feel an Angel, we must feel another's Heart,

To hear an Angel, we must listen to them both,

And...........................

To smell an Angel, you must know the perfume of Love!"

Feeling what is true is a sensate process and at a time when the great scales of the Universe shift to weigh our hearts and souls, we are encouraged and inspired to sense what is most pure, most true, most loving, and most morally advantageous for this time of divine reckoning - not just for now but forever!

We know 'truth' by the way it feels, and at times like these when we are bidden to move on from all that was once secure and dependable, we change because evolution is hard wired in our souls, and in our bio-chemistry. This reflects the self-managing, self-organizing principles of the Universe, for as we know after completion or death there is always resurrection and transcendence. Called by these subtle virtues we reach for the highest principles that can uplift us, those that are full of meaning, and those that have value to help us simply carry on, supported by their discernment, their everlasting efficacy and their divine connection.

Those of us who walk in devotion and dedication with the ancient traditions also feel the Sun, Moon and Stars deep within our cells, a communion fused within our Divine Blueprint. This experience leads us to determine a new hierarchy of values, underpinned by the ancient precepts that have always mattered, and as we do this let us also be led by the purest of beings who have always illuminated our paths – the Angels – for they come to calm and heal our feelings of disturbance with their love and joy, they come to recalibrate our earthly ways with the mind of heaven, they come to provide feeling intelligence for a better way of living, they come to strew our paths with rose petals. This is their higher vibrational eternal way of knowing, for they have seen bygone civilizations meeting similar fates as our own, and they know how we may shift, re-enervate and grow using what truly matters. Please let us all call upon them!

This is why Sophie's book is so significant for this time, it heals the mistaken belief that we are alone, and suggests such practical ways that we can make profound connection with the Angels as Cosmic Guardians. Enjoy your read!

Stewart Pearce

Angelic Emissary and Master of Voice

A Message From Sophie

My fascination for looking at the world from different perspectives began as a child. I discovered that I was highly sensitive to the energy given off by people and places, and often wonder if my impaired hearing allowed for my other senses to be heightened. I grew up with a paradox of being detached yet connected at a deeper level. This feeling has motivated my lifelong research into spirituality, knowing that there is more to life than what we can see. This deep understanding has driven my desire to connect people to the light and love of the Angels, and remind them of their natural, beautiful state.

Touring the temples in India, across the Himalayas to Bhutan and beyond, I was awakened to the beautiful high-frequency energy of these places. Here, people emitted a pure vibrancy that was calming and comforting to be around. The years I had spent learning and practising energy work, together with the beautiful intensity of these experiences, galvanised my focus even further.

Since then, I have gained masters qualifications in Angelic Reiki, having previously trained in Usui Reiki, all the while continuing to practise Indian head massage. My love of understanding the energetic realm has led me to becoming proficient in Numerology, and the connection between numbers and energy is a subject I find incredibly fascinating. I have also had a life-long love of colour, and indeed now live in a house named 'Rainbow House'. I've read countless books and attended various colour courses and seminars from personal colours in fashion to spiritual and energetic healing with colour. I trained with Kyle Gray to become a certified Angel card reader and Angel guide, and I began channelling my Angels and spirit guides through automatic writing.

I have trained with Tony Robbins on his Unleash The Power Within seminar, to gain further knowledge in keeping energy levels high. I advocate mindfulness and practise this daily while walking my dogs. Being with animals can teach us a lot about the importance of being fully present in the moment and the process of unconditional love.

This energetic sensitivity has developed to the extent that I now work with hands-on healing. I can tangibly feel the aura around people and feel when their chakras are blocked. I react energetically to others' energy around me, sensing and feeling their emotions before their body language or words have given them away. As a sentient light being, you are more than just the dense physical matter known as your body. Your energy radiates from you in what is known as your aura which can be in a state of contraction or expansion, in accordance with your state of mind, emotions and physical vitality. You may not realise it consciously, but you intuitively know who you resonate with on an energetic level just by feeling comfortable or not in their presence. You do this not just by the body language that they give out, but by the feeling of the energetic signature in their aura.

Learning to work with energy through methods such as visualisation, Reiki, colour, crystals, music and aroma has been my biggest passion in life, along with connecting people to the vast support team of Angels that surround them. I find it interesting that we are drawn to those with a strong sense of presence, who are comfortable to stand in their power. Their own light shines from within, and they become incandescent.

The cosmos is inside us and we have somewhere in the region of 50 trillion cells, which is more than all the stars in the Milky Way galaxy. In other words, within our bodies, there is a mirroring of the star system within the Milky Way. Your higher self is still connected to Source energy. You are a soul in a body, not a body in a soul. That connection is why, when we become more enlightened, we can tangibly feel that everything and everyone is connected, and fully understand that separation is the greatest illusion in this world. We are surrounded by Angels - beings of love and light - as well as friends and relatives who've passed over. We are all born with Guardian Angels dedicated to our wellbeing. We do not have to go through this life feeling that we are all on our own. Our energetic support team are only ever a thought away.

Every single one of us has suffered trauma of some variety. Even those who seemingly 'have it all' still have their fair share of pain to deal with. We come into this world forgetting that we are extensions of Source energy, also known as Chi, Prana, God or universal energy. The reality is that we are all far more powerful than we realise. My passion is to help you tap into that power, to release fear and connect back into the energy of love, which is your true essence of being.

This book is for anyone who wishes to raise their level of consciousness and gain a greater appreciation and understanding for life and all its complexities. You will be guided to have a better understanding of yourself and those around you as you learn to expand your compassion and self-worth.

It's my intention that in reading this you will have a greater sense of connection and awareness into the many strengths the Archangels have to offer us. It is my deepest passion that you will relate much more easily to the Angels after reading this book through direct examples that we all experience through life. When we work with these extraordinary Angels, their force is vast, but it is possible to bring the Angels into the ordinary countenance of our lives. In this book, I wanted to showcase their amazing powers in a way that is blended with practical day-to-day advice which can be used to build emotional resilience as well as mental and physical wellbeing. By following each Archangel and their area of expertise, you will discover a treasure trove of life-transforming exercises that will raise your vibration and bring you into alignment with the very best version of you.

CONTENTS

INTRODUCTION

Consider the kind of world your children will grow up in. What kind of future would you want for them and their future families? The world is developing at an incredibly fast pace from a technological standpoint, but is our consciousness accelerating at the same rate?

Over the last few decades, we have made tremendous strides in technical advancement, but our own safety and the progression of the planet has been held back. Until we develop the conscious maturity to manage the power it takes to advance us to the next level, we cannot move forward. As we continue to pollute the planet, threatening extinction to countless species, how can we elevate and raise human consciousness to become a society befitting of the technological progress? And with terrorist attacks and shootings occurring across the planet at an alarming rate, how can we raise human consciousness to realise that we are all one? How can we dissolve all perceived barriers of separation that play a fundamental role in halting our evolution?

The better we can communicate on a mass scale, the more we can cooperate with each other. This requires a fundamental understanding and acceptance of ourselves and others, where we suspend judgement. Judgement restricts, it can be cruel and it creates separation. What instead is required is unity consciousness where we bring about consideration, empathy, compassion and grace. This enables us to stay awake and keep learning in all the areas we can. The more we can spend time improving ourselves through meditation, connecting into the infinite power of universal Source energy, the quicker we can raise the vibration of this planet.

Right now, we are so commerce-driven that very few of us stop to consider how we can raise the state of humanity. External pressure to fit in, to have the right clothes and to continually achieve feed into the misguided belief that 'I am not enough'. We try and fill this void through consumerism – drugs, alcohol, sex and chasing dreams – believing that, 'When I have the car / job / partner / home / child / fortune ... then I will be happy.'

Many of us struggle with social anxiety, eating disorders, alcoholism, drug abuse, self-harming, depression and panic attacks, which all come down to the same belief – I am not enough. There is a void that is needed to be filled. The predominant collective consciousness of the planet at the moment is the feeling of 'what is the point?' There is a disconnection from ourselves as we seek happiness in external sources, leaving us wanting more. We all have a hunger, a longing for connection, a drive for a sense of purpose.

The intention of this book is to be of assistance in addressing that balance. My aspirations are that you will have a meaningful and fulfilling relationship with the Angels and a recognition of how they help you in every given moment, should you choose to acknowledge them. My own personal connection with the Angels gives me so much joy that sometimes I feel like my heart could quite literally burst! Watching synchronistic moments line up and the right people enter my life makes life feel like a magnificent dream. Hearing beautiful confirmation from the likes of the incredible Jan Costello as to how the Angels are supporting me just fills me with the deepest gratitude imaginable. It's this immeasurable joy and connection that I wish for you. Amidst all the struggling and difficulties, this incredible bliss is always available to us. Life should be magical for there are Divine forces conspiring to help us at every turn. My desire is that you invite them into your life so that you can be filled with the deep sense of love and peace that they provide.

Many of us believe that we are alone in this world, and this belief of separation is incredibly painful, sometimes to the point of suicidal thoughts. We are conceived in connection and our eternal perspective is that of oneness, so this visceral disconnection is a fall from grace. When we begin to see the world through the lens of me and everyone else and see ourselves as completely isolated from the world around us, we can be given a sense of separation, shame and fear. With the world as challenging as it can be, feelings of isolation and despair can sometimes feel overwhelming.

The reality is, however, that we are all an expression of source energy. We are connected to every sentient being in the universe. Most of us come into this life forgetting that we are a unique expression of divine universal consciousness, or Source energy. As we enter the Golden Age and we consciously evolve into a state of equality for all, we will be born with this realisation; the world will be a much more peaceful and nurturing place. We will have no need to compete; there will be no racism, sexism, ageism – everyone will be equal, existing in a state of utopia.

It is important to realise that our soul has chosen to come into this reality to experience all that is now. We did not come to this world expecting things to be better. We came here with the knowledge that everything is perfect just as it is. We came to remember who we really are, and experience the joy in that. We control our own reality. It is up to us to choose how we perceive what is going on around us. Our energy sets the tone for our experiences, as well as our expectations and beliefs.

Thankfully, the infinite number of Angels in existence help to bring us the hope, support and connection that we seek, ensuring our happiness and fulfilment. Angels are here to help us vibrate at a higher frequency, where feeling is the language of the soul. The whole of their language is feeling. The whole of the universe is based on the joy, delight and expansion of pure play. They do not have an experience of fear, scarcity or hatred. They are helping us to move forward into a world where love is stronger than fear, as we remember the truth of our divinity. At any moment, we have divine support and guidance available to us.

Guided by Angels was born from my passion to help others free themselves from pain and suffering using the power of connection with the Angels. In every moment, we have a spiritual support team around us, but it is up to us to open up and connect to it. I am well aware that life is a messy, and often painful process, and we all carry difficult emotions which affect our wellbeing. In some cases, these can be so crippling that we struggle to function. It is my intention that this book will be the stepping stone for you to connect with the divine for support, providing insight and understanding into why we feel the way we do, along with tips on how we can better support ourselves to live in our fullest potential. We are the creators of our world, and with the right focus and support, we are capable of anything.

This book has been created as an extension to my range of Angelic Energies scented healing mists (visit www.AngelicEnergies.co.uk for more information). These are an exquisite tool that can help you raise your vibration and connect to the love and support of the divine. I will be expanding on this towards the end of the book after Chapter 20 and the Guardian Angels.

Here you will find advice on how to gain emotional intelligence and develop emotional resilience. You will discover the importance of self-love and getting one's needs met. The driving force behind all of this inner strength is found in the connection to the divine for support. Separation is the greatest illusion in life, and we do not walk this path alone. Our Angels and guides are constantly providing messages of assistance and confirmation. We just have to realise that those niggling internal prompts are the whispers from our guides and Angels supporting us. We are all blessed with intuition; we just need to open up the space to listen to it, and have the courage to take action.

Our very essence is that of pure, unconditional love, and the Angels are here to remind us of that and bring us back into alignment with our true selves. The Archangels are infinite beings of pure unconditional love. Just as with human expression, each Archangel has their own unique abilities and characteristics, and so by getting to know them, we can forge a greater connection. When we encounter challenges and difficulties in our lives, we can more easily navigate to calmer shores by calling on our support team for help. Just like with humans, when a call for help is made to a specific person, it's much more likely to be answered than if it went out to the collective. Therefore, targeting an individual Archangel is guaranteed to get their support.

Throughout this book, we will be getting to know the Archangels on a much deeper level, by diving into Angelic psychological insight given to me by my guides. I am deeply blessed to be working in accordance with the Angels, and to be able to share their love and support with you here. You will be given practical life tips to assist you in overcoming a broad spectrum of challenges and difficulties that we all face throughout our existence in this 3D reality on Earth.

It is also my intention that the insights for each Archangel in this book have relatable real-life concepts that will help you to formulate new beliefs and practises. The beliefs we hold true have a massive effect on the way we go through life. Beliefs are the present, organised filters to our perception of the world. Beliefs are usually created by what we experience or what others tell us to be true and they are the guiding principles in life that provide direction and meaning in life. When we change our thinking, we change our beliefs. When we change our beliefs, we change our behaviour. By consciously integrating your spirit rather than simply intellectually stimulating yourself, you will become more of who you are as you ground spirit as deeply as possible into your everyday life. You do this through feeling and bringing your emotions to your awareness. By deciding ahead of time what you desire to feel, you become the master of your own destiny.

I hope that this book helps you to better understand yourself, and give you the courage to express and meet your needs. We all have needs, and we must find a way for these needs to be met. We are all valuable and worthy of happiness – it's our birth right. When we become conscious creators of our universe, we become far more powerful than we could ever realise, only if we can stop fear from blocking us. Fear will always be there, and if your dreams don't scare you then they're not big enough. But we don't have to let fear rule the show; we can accept it for what it is and instead choose to focus on our reasons why. We can allow fear to galvanise us into action. When fear is present, it can be a sign that we are passionate about what we're doing. We can never totally get rid of it, so we need to embrace it and take it with us along our journey.

We all strive to make a positive difference to humanity, across all nations and races. Every single person is on this planet for a reason, and we all have something valuable to contribute. I hope this book brings greater understanding to the human state so that we can feel empowered to know that we are all enough. We do not walk this path alone; we are all connected – to each other, our Angels, our guides and ancestors. We are all supported by our Angels, who hold the vision of us as a perfect divine being of love and light. It is my hope that you will be lifted up to step into that light, and shine for the world to see!

Guided By Angels

PART 1:
CONNECTING WITH THE ANGELS

CHAPTER 1:
CONNECTING WITH THE ANGELS

*'Angels are the thoughts, the memory, the sensation of love.
They are whatever comes and shifts us from being lost within
ourselves, to seeing again, not with the ego, but with the heart.'*
~ Mary Magdalene
('Mary Magdalene Revealed' by Meggan Watterson)

A ngels are the highest vibrational guides that exist on all dimensions. Angels are messengers from God who are here to connect us to our Source energy, to our higher selves, to guide us towards our own enlightenment and remember our own divinity. Angels must be invited to be part of our conscious awareness and reality. They hold the space in their beautiful high vibrational state for us to remember our own divinity and to be able to raise our own vibration and feelings of oneness. They respond to the vibration of what we are choosing to do with our life. If we are immersed in drama, they will leave us alone and give us the space to move out of that state. When we choose to shift away from drama and move into a space of healing, the Angels come in with state of love; the highest vibration known to us. The most astonishing thing is that their lowest feeling state is something we call ecstasy. If you want to connect with the Angels you must simply set that intention. Invite them in and ask for guidance or any question you have.

The Angels are there to help us with resolving our issues. They are helping us to resolve our negativity, to resolve our karma. They are helping resolve our attachments to weight, space and time. They are helping us to absolve from our perception of loss, so that we can recognise that there can be no loss. Even if we are alone, that is not a loss, it's an opportunity to be glorious with solitude, so that we can develop an even greater conversation with the divine. This is because the way to really access the Divine lies in the stillness, not in action. We can have conversations through prayer, meditation, through chant and through states of relaxation or when we allow our mind to quieten.

After asking for help for your highest good, tune in and see if you can feel their energy and presence. Trust that, even if you don't feel anything, they are with you. Once you've asked for their support and guidance, pay attention to any signs and messages.

Angels can communicate in many different ways. You can become aware of them through signs, such as 11.11, that carry their high frequency of light. They give their reassurance through us finding feathers or coins in unusual places. We may find the right book we need for specific advice at the right time, or catch a song lyric that is pertinent to how we are feeling. You may notice sudden changes of temperature, or have the feeling of your hair standing on end. A friend of mine always gets goose bumps when Angels are around and we call them Angel bumps! Some people are lucky enough to get a full blown visual of an Angelic being. I myself see them as orbs of coloured light in meditation while I am giving a healing, or flickers of golden light while out walking.

My favourite way to connect with the Angels is through Angel cards. The cards never fail to amaze me on the accuracy of their guidance. I highly recommend that you find a deck that resonates with you and use them on a daily basis. Find a deck where the artwork really speaks to you. I have a huge basket full of card decks, but only a small selection of personal favourites. I use the Angel Tarot by Radleigh Valentine and Doreen Virtue, and the Frequency Tarot by Teal Swan which give me fantastic insight. I am also a big fan of cards by Alana Fairchild and Sandra Anne Taylor.

It is with huge excitement that I can announce that I have created for you the *Guided By Angels Oracle Cards* to accompany this book. The 54-card deck and guidebook bring you messages that can help you heal every area of your life! The information they bring through will empower and inspire you to take decisive steps based on those answers. There are no negative cards in this deck, since the Angels always counsel us from a place of love. In this oracle card set you will find three powerful uplifting messages from each of the 16 Archangels mentioned in this book, along with three loving messages from your Guardian Angels, and three transformational 'I AM' affirmation cards. All that you need to support your spiritual growth and wellbeing is available to you, so let your intuition soar, listen to the messages it brings, and take your life to wonderful new heights! These empowering, uplifting cards with artwork from James Howells, are available from www.AngelicEnergies.co.uk.

Take the time to familiarise yourself with your selected deck and look at each card individually. Bless them and ask that they be messengers for the highest good. Then, after shuffling, close your eyes, hold them up to your heart, and say, 'Thank you, Angels, for revealing to me what I need to know.' Pick a card for yourself every day and keep them in a prominent position near to where you sleep so that they can absorb your energy. My cards have become like my best friends, giving me immense comfort and guidance.

In my healing practise, I have developed the Angelic Energies Ritual which includes an aura cleanse, chakra balance with crystals, and blissful Angelic Reiki. As part of that practise, I will share with you my favourite healing meditation that I use which harnesses the help of the Archangels to cleanse and balance the seven main chakras.

As an added extra to this book, there are audio recordings of the meditations available for you to enjoy on a private page of my website. To listen, please enter into your browser the following address www.angelicenergies.co.uk/guided-meditations. From there, please enter the password to access your meditations.

Password: Angels

While listening, I encourage you to put as much emotion into connecting with your feelings as you can.

MEDITATION TO CONNECT TO SEVEN ARCHANGELS WHILE REBALANCING THE CHAKRAS

Here is beautiful guided meditation to connect to these seven Archangels as we remove any negative energy from our chakras (the seven wheels of energy that spin within our body). The flow of this energy starts at the base of the spine, known as the base or root chakra, and continues upwards to the top of the head, known as the crown chakra.

Get yourself comfortable. Take a deep breath in, filling up your belly, and then exhale fully, knowing that in this moment, you are entering a very safe, peaceful state in your heart, mind and body. Breathe in, and allow yourself to let go as you breathe out, relaxing deeper. In this moment, you are safe to relax. It doesn't matter what is going on around you, or within you emotionally. Know that it is safe for you to relax, unload, and connect inwards.

Slowly breathe in and out. Take your time, not rushing to achieve a specific state. Just knowing that all you have to do is be here and now. Relax your facial muscles and your jaw. Breathing in, and breathing out.

Focus your attention on your base or root chakra (located just at the bottom of your spine), and on the soles of your feet. Feel yourself connecting to the energy of the earth and all the energy that the earth provides. Imagine that you are surrounded by a bright red light now, and picture a red spinning disk turning in a clockwise direction here. Call in Archangel Uriel now to help ground your energy, and help you to create a solid foundation to be able to open up the other chakras. The base chakra relates to the feeling of stability, strength, safety and survival. Continue to imagine a red spinning disk here, and affirm to yourself, 'I am peaceful, protected and secure. All my needs are met.' Tune in now to the vibration of excitement, and feel how that resonates through your body.

Now, move your focus up to the sacral chakra, which can be found just above the pubic bone and just below the navel. Imagine a fuchsia pink light as we call in Archangel Chamuel, the Angel of love and passion, to help clear any negative energy that may be blocking this area. While still breathing in and out, picture an orange disk spinning in a clockwise direction over your sacral chakra. This chakra relates to our consciousness of our emotions, and relates to our feelings and passions. This chakra is for our sexuality and how we relate to the world. You have much more scope to be creative than you may realise. Any time you garden, bake or cook, you are creating. You create when you find new solutions to old problems. Anytime you take materials and turn them into something else, you are creating. Picture this orange disk spinning and affirm to yourself, 'I am radiant, beautiful and strong, and enjoy a healthy and passionate life.' Tune in now to the frequency of joy and focus on the creator energy. Feel how that resonates through your body.

We are continuing up to the solar plexus chakra, which can be found around your belly. This chakra is related to courage, confidence and willpower. Imagine this area surrounded with golden light as we call in Archangel Jophiel to help heal our emotions and feelings of worthiness. Picture a yellow spinning disk here and affirm to yourself, 'I embody confidence and inner peace. I am worthy and deserving of everything I desire in life, and I set boundaries with ease and self-respect.' Tune in now to the vibration of confidence. Feel how that resonates through your body.

Next, we move to the heart chakra, which can be found in the centre of the chest and relates to unconditional love, compassion and wellbeing. Picture an emerald green light around this area and call in Archangel Raphael, the master healer, to clear your sacred heart. Picture a vibrant green disk spinning in a clockwise direction. Archangel Raphael supports all living forms of life. When your sacred heart is filled with love and light, you will not feel needy, manipulative or demanding. When you love and respect yourself, you will be authentic, happy and empowered as you are filled with the grace of courage. Continue to picture this beautiful vibrant green disk spinning, and affirm to yourself, 'Love is the answer to everything in life, and I give and receive love effortlessly and unconditionally.' Tune in now to the frequency of compassion. Feel how that resonates through your body.

We are moving up now to the throat chakra, which can be found at the base of your throat. Picture a cobalt blue light here, and imagine a spinning disk in sky blue. This chakra is governed by Archangel Michael who, with his sword of truth and scales of justice, can help us release criticism, unkind words and harsh judgement. We ask him to be with us now as we ask for his assistance in helping us express and communicate clear thoughts and ideas. Michael's grace enables us to give and receive wise council, and speak our truth as we clear this chakra. Continue to imagine this sky-blue disk spinning and affirm to yourself, 'My thoughts are positive, and I always express myself truthfully and clearly.' Tune in now to the vibration of freedom. Feel how that resonates through your body.

Now, bring your attention down to your third eye, located in the centre of the forehead, right between the eyebrows. Picture a deep blue indigo disk spinning here. Now imagine a violet light surrounding this area as we call in Archangel Zadkiel. This powerful Archangel will help you release all shadows, behaviours and patterns that you deny seeing in yourself or others around you. Imagine a violet light that flows, and as it does, it brings clear sight and helps you improve all of your 'clairs', especially your clairvoyance and claircognisance. You are now open to the grace of love and understanding. Continue to imagine this deep blue indigo disk spinning, and affirm to yourself, 'I am tuned into the divine universal wisdom, and I always understand the true meaning of life situations.' Tune in now to the vibration of power. Feel how that resonates through your body.

Bring your awareness to your crown chakra, by focusing your attention on the top of your head. Imagine now a beautiful white light here as you picture a violet disk spinning in a clockwise direction. With this white light comes Archangel Gabriel, the messenger Angel. Invite this magnificent Angel of the pure white ray of divine light to open your crown chakra, strengthening your connection to the divine. With this energy, he brings clarity, peacefulness, inspiration, creativity and joy. We ask Archangel Gabriel to clear away any negative thoughts that are blocking our soul from feeling the love, wisdom and communication for our higher self. Continue to imagine this violet disk spinning, and affirm to yourself, 'I am complete and one with the Divine energy.' Tune in now to the vibration of expansion and connection. Feel how that resonates through your body.

Now, imagine your whole body cocooned in golden Angelic light, and notice that your aura has expanded out as you feel your chakras bling with energy. Thank these Archangels now as you bring your awareness back into this space, back into the now. Visualise silver roots coming from your feet deep down into the ground as you give yourself a stretch. Take a deep breath and come back into your body, and open your eyes.

CALLING ON THE ANGELS

Due to free will, you must consciously focus on Angels for them to become a part of your subjective reality. They cannot impose themselves upon you. Ask for help or an answer to a question, and then let go. Nothing is trivial to them, so never be afraid to ask for their support. Their expansion relies on our connection to them. We are their soul purpose. The Archangels are omnipresent beings, capable of being everywhere at the same time, meaning that by calling on them, we never detract from someone else getting assistance. They can be with any number of people in any place at the same time.

The simplest way to connect to your Angels is to ask them something and involve them in all aspects of your life. For example; I have made it a habit that every time I hear an ambulance, I always say, 'May the Angels be with you.' I visualise Angelic energy surrounding the speeding vehicle. When I can't find what I'm looking for, I ask Archangel Chamuel, who is all-seeing, to help me find the item. When I am running late, I ask Archangel Metatron - who has the power over time - to freeze it for me. When I am in pain, I ask assistance from Archangel Raphael who helps with pain control. It is useful to know what each Archangel specialises in in order to ask for specific help, and I will be sharing more about this later in this book. Just asking in general for the Angels' guidance and assistance is enough, though. If ever I am worried about anything, my first response is to ask for Angelic assistance; immediately, I feel a sense of peace wash over me.

It is important to gain awareness and power over thoughts, as they influence our vibrational set point that creates the reality we live in. The world is our mirror. Attaining a shift in focus to experience the harmony, joy and peace that we all desire may not be so easy when you're in a state of pain. In this book, we will talk about the importance of sitting with difficult emotions and not distracting, avoiding or numbing them. Upsetting emotions need to be validated, and only then can they be transformed. When we feel that it's not acceptable to feel the way that we do, forcing ourselves to feel a different way, we suffer more as a result. It's important to fully acknowledge how you feel and why, and then ask the Angels for assistance. They are always listening and want to help, but they operate based on free will, so they cannot intervene unless you ask them for assistance. That little voice inside your head is the Angels giving you guidance as to what to do next. You are never alone. Guidance and support are always on hand. Find a quiet time to listen and, most importantly, take action when guidance is given.

CHAPTER 2:
DIVINE GUIDANCE

'It does not matter how long you are spending on the Earth, how much money you have gathered, or how much attention you have received. It is the amount of positive vibration you have radiated in life that matters.' - Amit Ray

This is the mantra I dedicated my life to practise. I, like many, have experienced a great deal of sorrow and pain, and have come through this with the help from my Guardian Angels, Angels and Archangels, and the strength and support they have shared. I'm passionate about helping you make a shift in consciousness and recognise the true divine spirit that you are. You are a spark of universal Source energy, or God if you prefer. It's not something outside of you, so don't be scared to embrace your true power. Anything and everything is possible with the help of your Angels.

Angels are here to remind us of our true divine essence of pure unconditional love. We are so blessed to be living in a time when the concept of Angels, Guardian Angels and Archangels are well documented and understood. Diana Cooper, Stewart Pearce, Radleigh Valentine, Jacky Newcomb, Kyle Gray, Chrissie Astell and

Lorna Byrne, and Calista Ascension with the Female Archangels have been leading lights in this field, to name a few. We now understand Angels to be non-human spiritual beings that are the energy of God, or the One Universal Source of Intelligence, each with distinct personalities and specialist skills. The sole purpose of the Angels is to support us through life, lifting us higher to be able to achieve our full potential.

All of us have (and will) face challenging times in our lives. I believe we choose the life we are born into, so that we may grow and evolve. It was no accident that we have the family we do. This is our soul group that has agreed to connect through many lifetimes. We have specific lessons to learn and problems to overcome, and none of us are assured an easy ride, no matter how privileged we may be. It is through these challenges that we experience the contrast between where we are and where we want to be, which causes us to expand and grow. In this world of duality, by knowing what we don't want, we can clearly know what we do.

Desire is the primary motivational force that allows us to evolve. As mentioned, this is based on knowing what we don't want. This point of contrast causes you to feel the need to transcend. Without being lost, we do not know what it means to find ourselves. Hemingway stated that, 'We are all broken. That's how the light gets in.' It is through great moments of darkness that our soul is reawakened to head towards the light. Otherwise, we would drift along, never challenging ourselves or knowing what we are truly capable of.

Our soul's purpose is to expand and grow. We are all continually striving and wanting more. The secret to happiness is to enjoy the process. There is no point in thinking, 'I'll be happy when...' There will always be something else to reach out for. Decide to be happy now. We came into this world to experience the joy of creating our desires and watching them transpire – 'There is just as much satisfaction to be had in the anticipation of knowing that what you are seeking is seeking you.' (Rumi).

By contrast, in the Heavenly world, we feel entirely safe and at peace as we experience the merging with others and the feelings of unconditional love. There is no ego, no body, and nothing to protect. We have no race, gender, religion, culture, or any other limiting categories. As limitless beings of pure love and light, our thoughts and feelings create instant reactions. There is no constriction of time and space. Manifestation is instantaneous, and challenges do not exist.

We are all born with this beautiful pure love and light, and no matter what happens, we will die with this love and light and return to Source energy. Our only task in this life is to honour our true authentic self. And to do this, we must live in alignment with our values. The direction we take in life comes from our values as they are the emotional states that we believe are important to either experience or avoid. They determine every thought, emotion and experience we have, so it's important to be consciously aware of our values and prioritise them accordingly.

When we don't know what they are, life throws a series of hard knocks, so we learn what we want through knowing what we don't want to experience anymore. Values should fill us with integrity and pride and give us a strong core. By being consciously aware of our values, we know what things mean to us. Strong emotions are always connected to a value.

Notice how you are acting and the decisions you are making and see if they are in alignment. Values may change over time, and that's fine. There is little point thinking that you'll change how things are in the future, as now is the only moment the universe responds to. Things will always be the same with that mentality. If changes need to be made, be decisive and adjust now.

The Angels want you to understand that there are no limits, and anything is possible. You are incapable of desiring something that is not meant to be yours. You are incapable of thinking a thought that is not intended to come to fruition. If you want it, it must be. We are the only thing that stands in the way of our success and happiness.

CHAPTER 3:
GETTING TO KNOW YOUR ANGELS

Questioner: 'How should I treat others?'
Ramana Maharshi: 'There are no others.'

Separation is the greatest illusion in life. In reality, we are all connected. Becoming spiritually aware is to remember our true identity as limitless light beings of unconditional love, connected to everything and everyone. True strength and bliss can be felt in connecting back into that Source energy, and the best way to do that is through meditation. Making a conscious effort to sit in silence every day, focusing on our breath and letting our thoughts drift by without attachment, is one of the most beneficial things we can do. It is in this moment, when we are tapped into Source or universal energy, that everything is available to us. Creative insights flow as we are given thoughts to catapult ourselves forward. Synchronistic moments can then occur, and the right people to help us start to show up.

Having an acceptance and openness to what the Angels can guide us towards - and a willingness to follow - can open up life to unimaginable, infinite possibilities. Our heart becomes fuller, and we are filled with inner confidence, wonder and excitement. We are, after all, unlimited beings. What would you do if you knew you couldn't fail? We need to be continually challenging ourselves to grow. That is our purpose for being here. So many of us have incredible ideas, yet what we think is missing is motivation. That's not true. What is holding us back is the fear of failure. Our brains are designed to protect us from things that are scary, uncomfortable or difficult, but to achieve something, we need to be able to overcome these feelings. The Angels can give us the courage and support to follow our dreams, to face our fears, and to move forward every day.

The express purpose of the Angels is to help you to experience peace, joy, health and happiness. The Angels have to respect our free will, so they can only help you if you ask them to or give them permission. It doesn't matter how you ask, so long as you do.

This book is an expansion on the concept of Angelic Energies' Scented Healing Mists, giving greater detail on how the seven Archangels of the seven rays can assist us. It also incorporates nine further Archangels. There are countless Angels in existence, but here we shall be focusing on the sixteen most well-known Archangels.

PART 2:
THE ARCHANGELS

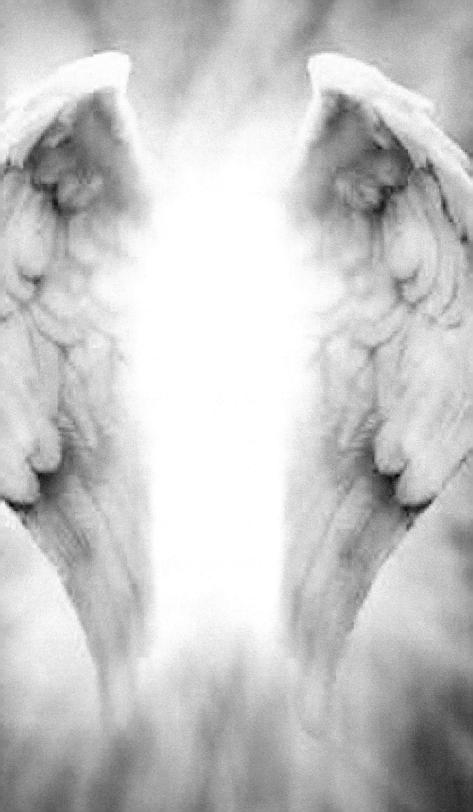

THE ARCHANGELS

The Archangels are omnipresent beings, so they are not limited to space and time. They are capable of being with many people across the whole world, giving different messages at any given moment. Angels want us to be peaceful and happy, and will do anything they can to help us live a more harmonious life. The four most well-known Archangels through Christianity and Judaism, are:

Archangel Michael - in the South with the element Fire

Archangel Raphael - in the East with the element Air

Archangel Gabriel - in the West with the element Water

Archangel Uriel - in the North with the element Earth

This book does not come from a man-made religious standpoint, however. This next section will provide a full break-down of each of the 16 Archangels mentioned here, to include their purpose, and how they can specifically help you when called upon. Where applicable, I have included details of the appropriate healing mist, blended to assist you in connecting with the Archangel.

Guided By Angels

30

CHAPTER 4:
ARCHANGEL MICHAEL

Strength, Courage, Protection and Life Purpose

Super Powers   Strength / Motivation / Courage / Protection
/ Fixing electrical items / Life Purpose /
Confidence / Worthiness / Self-Esteem

Name Translation   He who is like God

Crystal   Sugilite

Colour   Electric cobalt blue and gold

Helping People   Emergency Services, light workers, psychic
protection with cord cutting.

Ray   1st Blue Ray of protection and power

Archangel Michael, perhaps the most well-known, comes in on the 1st ray and is the Angelic director of the blue ray, the ray of protection, faith, and the will of God. So, it's no wonder that Michael is known as the divine protector. The crystal associated with him is sugilite. By wearing the blue crystal sugilite, you may find yourself channelling profound and loving statements from Michael.

Michael will grant you freedom from fear, keeping you safe and giving energy and vitality. He can also be handy at fixing electrical items. This is because in today's modern times, technology is part of everything we do. When it goes wrong, it causes us great distress, and the Angels want nothing more than to help us lead a peaceful and harmonious life. There have been countless stories where people have asked Archangel Michael for assistance with their broken down car, only to have him save the day.

Michael helps with all aspects of life purpose and increases motivation, worthiness, confidence, and self-esteem. He can guide your next step, help you to make significant life changes, and gain support in knowing your life purpose.

Archangel Michael's name means 'He who is Like God', and he can soothe our fears and assist in situations where we are afraid, confused, or concerned for our safety. With his sword of light, he allows us to let go of feelings that are no longer serving us by releasing fear and doubt. This sword can also sever unwanted connections to the past or to people we feel the need to be safely and lovingly removed from our life. This may sound drastic, but if a person has a hold over you and is draining you, it's necessary to regain your own power. Following a divorce or separation, it's really important that the energetic cords that held you together are cut, enabling you to move on with your life.

I highly recommend adopting a daily spiritual practise of connecting to Archangel Michael and asking for his psychic protection. Your aura is like a sponge. As you go through the day, you absorb the surrounding energy of emails, the news, screaming children and people off-loading onto you. It takes two minutes to simply ask Michael to cut the cords of people, places or situations that no longer serve you. I link this to an activity that I do every day so that I don't forget to do it. For me, it's in the shower at the end of the day. Water is a great purifier which adds to this ritual. You may prefer to do this while brushing your teeth, if that works better for you. You can also imagine his essence - his energy - cocooning you in his cobalt blue light.

I'd like to share with you a beautiful poem written by an amazing woman called Ronnie Williams.

IN GRATITUDE

Archangel Michael please enter my day
And let it work out in a wonderful way
Archangel Michael please enter my day
Chasing the shadows and darkness away
Please enter my heart and enter my mind,
Let me leave doubt and worry behind.
Let me find happiness, let me find peace:
Let all my worry and anxiety cease.
I open up to receive your love
Flowing freely from above.
I place myself within your light
Where all is healed and all comes right,
Filled with grace I know I am free
To live my life abundantly.

Archangel Michael, as He Who Is Like God, can be thought of as the leader of the Angelic Kingdom. I find it fascinating to discover through communication with Stewart Pearce, that the Archangels do not wish to be considered to be as a hierarchy. They explained to him that the term hierarchy used to mean governance of the sacred, but actually hierarchy has changed in its vibration and is now associated with patriarchy. Archangel Michael can be thought of as the protector of those that feel called to heal this world – light workers, the police force and emergency services. As their role is to protect the public, it's natural that Michael will be protecting them.

Archangel Michael is probably the most popular of all the Archangels. I know when I ask people if they have a favourite Angel, the majority answer Michael. He has an amazing presence that appeals to so many channellers, mediums, and light workers. As an omnipresent being, along with all the other Archangels, Michael's energy is multi-dimensional; he is capable of being with any person in any place or time. His wonderful energy makes us feel safe, secure and protected.

I learned a wonderful trick from my dear friend, Carrie. If ever I was worried about the safety of anything, I could simply imagine placing three gold rings of protection around it. She knew that we create our own reality, and by removing fear, we can elevate ourselves out of danger. This handy trick has never failed for me. I can remember walking through my local park one afternoon. No one else was around. The next thing I knew, three youths in hooded tops appeared, walking along the path in my direction. I instantly felt threatened and fearful. In that moment, I energetically felt the presence of my belated Grandma's huge big dog beside me. This huge bullmastiff had the presence of a lion. I completely relaxed and went on my way. As I did so, the youths turned the corner and went the other way.

Over time, Archangel Michael has been seen with a bluish light, which is either a deep purple or a cobalt. The presence of Archangel Michael can often bring heat as he is sometimes known as the Angel of Fire, and he is associated with the direction of East, where the sun rises. You may like to imagine him as a gigantic blue energy with roaring flames, capable of burning away fear. It's interesting to note that we naturally associate the colour blue to authority and those in a position of trust. A great tip, if you're going for a job interview, is to wear the colour navy blue. Psychologically, you're perceived as more trustworthy, and so your chances of success are greatly boosted.

Start your day with Angelic protection and healing prayer to protect yourself from lower energies, and choose to surround yourself with universal love. Ask Archangel Michael to protect you with a sphere of white light from the top of your head to the tip of your toes. Fill that sphere of white light with love, harmony, protection and healing. Keep that white light free from any negative energies. Expand that sphere of white light to the space that you are in at all times. Ask that this white light shine unconditional love and healing to everyone around you. May the appropriate helpers from the Universe be with you in everything that you do now, and for all days to come.

Your home can also be given protection. You can imagine your home is surrounded by a sphere of light, or the three gold rings. Again, fill that sphere of light with protection, unconditional love, harmony and healing. Visualise shining light and unconditional love to every corner of every room of your home. If ever you are worried about anything, just imagine it surrounded in light and know that it will be safe.

I conduct space clearing for people, which disperses stuck energy and spirits, harmonising the home and making things feel lighter and brighter. As I do this, I ask for each room to be filled with love and light and positive vibration. Your home should be a sanctuary where you feel safe and at peace. If there are circumstances beyond your control that make it otherwise, set the intention to move and find your perfect sanctuary.

Navigating our way through the dense physical environment of this world can feel awkward and clumsy as we are weighed down by the practical physical reality of life. Our automatic response to this pressure can be one of fear. This occurs as we live by our limited physical senses, where feelings of insecurity, self-doubt, being afraid and worrying what other people think of us may arise. Our conditioning is not designed to help us with this because it is naturally wired to try and protect us from things that are scary, uncomfortable or difficult. This serves us well when we are doing practical things like crossing a road, but when we need to be proactive, e.g. asking for a promotion or pay rise, we often hesitate. At that moment, our brain produces all manner of reasons why we can't achieve something. Fear has won and stopped us in our tracks. We are, however, here to grow and evolve, and in doing so, we need to push ourselves past our comfort zones and embrace challenges continuously. Remember, the universe wants you to succeed, and when you call on the Angels for help along the way, you can transform every situation as you realise your dreams.

Research through the American Scientific Association discovered that, out of the 60,000 thoughts we have on average each day, 50,000 of those are negative. This was discovered by the secretion of hormones and the work has been stated in the book by Daniel Goldman entitled *Emotional Intelligence.* High achievers often condition themselves to believe that they are excited so that they can move past the feelings of fear and get on and succeed in what they are doing. By telling yourself that you have chosen to do this and that you feel great about it, you override the fear that holds you back.

LIFE PURPOSE

If you need self-confidence or clarity on your life purpose, call upon Michael. He can help you feel like you're getting your life back on track. Many of us confuse our life purpose with what we do for a career. These are not necessarily the same thing. I have a huge love for Numerology, a practise that dates back two thousand years. The premise is that every number carries different energy; relating your full birth name and date of birth, and breaking these down to single digits, provides a lot of insightful personal information. In this way, we each carry our own individual blueprint of what we need to do to feel fulfilled in this lifetime. We can also discover where our talents lie, how others perceive us, understand precipice turning points in our lives and karmic lessons, and much more. In writing personal numerology reports for others, I never fail to be amazed at the level of detail it provides to get under the skin of what makes people tick. It's fascinating to do this for babies too to gain insight into the personality they will go on to develop.

YOUR LIFE PATH NUMBER IN NUMEROLOGY

The Life Path number is the most important one in Numerology as it is said to uncover what you need to do in this lifetime to feel fulfilled. This is the ruling force that describes what you must do in order to operate harmoniously with your environment and get the most out of your life. It is calculated by adding the full date of birth. You will also be given insight here into why your soul chose to incarnate as this particular life path and what your soul is hoping to achieve by doing so.

The Life Path number is calculated by adding all the digits in a date of birth until they reach a single digit. For example; September 14th, 1956, would be:

$9 + 1 + 4 + 1 + 9 + 5 + 6 = 35$

$3 + 5 = 8$

Please note: if your end number comes to 11, please do not reduce this further as 11 is classed as a master number with its own special vibration.

To see if you're in alignment with your soul's life purpose, here is a summary of each of the different life path numbers.

LIFE PATH NUMBER ONE

Number One, as you might imagine, is about new beginnings.

Normally the soul will choose a number one life path when the previous life has been one in which a lot of loose ends have been tied up. The life immediately before this one has often been chaotic and fragmented. Now the soul is ready to start a new phase, much like finishing one book and beginning another. Number One is quite an important life path because whatever is done in this life will lay the foundations for the next sequence of lives.

In this lifetime, the soul wants to establish a direction for the future. For this reason, Number One people will find a clear focus on their priorities. You can be incredibly single-minded, focused and independent, achieving impressive things. With One as your Life Path Number, you are sure to succeed substantially. However, you may have blind spots and naivety can trip you up. It can be a shock to find that someone has not carried out the tasks that they have been given in the same dedicated way that you would. Every so often, your life may fall apart (or seem to), but like a phoenix you always rise up from the ashes and soar towards the sky, leaving a trail of sparks in your wake.

You have a feeling that you stand and fall by your own efforts. It is not that you don't trust others or that you have no one to help you, and it doesn't mean that you do everything yourself. There will be tasks and activities that are outside your range of skills, and you are only too happy to hand these over. But deep down, you know that you are not going to be the person you want and need to be if you don't do something yourself.

It is important that you choose a path in life that enables you to make your mark in a unique way. Be courageous and do things your way. It's important for you to always have a result to aim for. Having a sense of achievement is everything to you. You do need to ensure that you are not too driven, and one way to achieve this is to set balance and adequate rest as one of your goals.

Tips for Number Ones:

- Be organised and create a list of what you want to complete each day. If you don't complete everything, carry it forward to the next day.

- Consciously set high aims and review your progress.

LIFE PATH NUMBER TWO

Number Two is the number of duality. As you walk through life, you need a partner in everything you do. On this life path, the soul is choosing to look in the mirror – what better way is there of doing this than being in a relationship! In relationships, the soul has its unconscious self reflected in others.

Being in a relationship can be a great thing or a recipe for heartache and frustration – it all depends on how good you are at choosing. You seek to please and have a high regard for the welfare of others, even though you might not tend to think of yourself highly. There is a danger that you could be used, and become dominated by a more demanding personality. This could happen if you lose sight of reality and think the relationship is everything instead of moving in tandem towards a shared goal.

So, what sort of 'shared goal' might fulfil you? Something that generates love and compassion outside the narrow orbit of personal concerns. Something that involves balance, peace and harmony. The theme of self-awareness and true perception runs throughout. Even though you may feel strongly about diplomacy and tolerance, occasionally you can be pitched to take sides. Once forced to enter the fray, you may see yourself in a position where you can only win or lose, fighting blindly and jeopardising your achievements and peace of mind. There is no need for this – your challenge is always to see the connections and raise things to a level where conflicts are not so much resolved as irrelevant.

It's crucial for you to have the correct support in whatever you do, so ensure this is in place. Your first responsibility must always be to protect yourself and your vulnerabilities. Only from a position of strength will you be able to help others. This is not the easiest life path for the soul as you will be bringing things to light that have previously been too difficult to face. Your soul has realised the tendency to put a lid on your emotions and feelings, and it has chosen this life path for you to open up. You are here to learn to co-operate with other people such as co-workers, children, friends and partners. You are a very sensitive soul and will sometimes find life a bit 'too much' to handle, wanting to retreat to a place where you do not have to face your demons. Know that if you have chosen isolation, you are running away from the purpose of this life path, so have the courage to come out of hiding.

Tips for Number Twos:

- If you're feeling hurt, talk about this to a trusted friend. Another perspective always helps.

- Take time out to meditate and get in touch with your intuition.

- Always have something to nurture.

LIFE PATH NUMBER THREE

Expressing yourself and creating something that gives others pleasure is your primary drive. Enabling other people to communicate and move their lives onwards is a major motivation for you. You see yourself as making the world a better place. Being able to act spontaneously is important to you – freedom allows you to follow serendipitous moments in life.

There is great joy in living, but it is not enough for you to experience this – you want to inspire it. You may develop the gift of persuasive rhetoric so that you can charm the birds out of the trees, but you also like to hear other people speaking their thoughts and ideas. You are likely a great brain stormer and in your element when you feel something fabulous is just around the corner.

Sometimes you may feel that, however much you say, you are not really heard; however much happiness you spread, you have not done quite enough. You have a 'divine discontent' that can spur you on. There is always something more to explore. Other people may think that you are never satisfied, but you are mostly just enjoying the journey.

You need to choose a path that will give you flexibility and opportunities to free that creative spirit within you. There is a danger of you not being grounded and you can be too much in the head and prone to being easily led. Spiritual discipline is especially important to keep balance, and practises such as Tai Chi, martial arts or Yoga can be of huge benefit.

Often, a soul who has chosen a Life Path Three has recently emerged from a past life devoid of spirituality, and has now chosen to explore their divine consciousness. Choosing this life path, the soul is moving towards understanding its place and purpose in the greater whole. The purpose is to learn that divinity is not 'out there' but is within everything that exists.

Tips for Number Threes:

- Express any talent you have (music, poetry, writing). Just because it comes easily does not mean it is not worth developing.

- Play is a serious business. Children learn through it, and so do you, so make time for it.

- Always have a project on the go – better to start something and change your mind than not to do anything.

LIFE PATH NUMBER FOUR

You like to do things in the correct order. This means you set yourself milestones of achievement and do things 'on schedule' – go to university, get a job, get married, have kids, all in that order and at the right time.

As a Four, you are the dedicated worker of the world. We turn to

Fours when we need organisation in our life and to understand how things work. Fours are practical, determined, organised and structured. They are very hardworking, honest and have good old-fashioned morals.

The challenges you may face include being intolerant, inflexible and controlling of your environment. You are very home loving, love your family, and need emotional and physical stability.

You are usually good at saving money and making it go a long way. If possible, you will have your life mapped out, determined to proceed from birth to death in an orderly fashion. You are aware of your abilities and trust your knowledge and experience, but sometimes your calm exterior is little more than skin deep, feeling anxious about potential disasters. If things don't go to plan, however, you manage very well, reverting to plan B. In fact, you cope with real trouble much better than you do with the imaginary kind.

You will probably be happiest dealing with practical things – fantasy and emotion can be too distracting. If something is not useful, or will not enhance your creature comforts (or those of your loved ones or humanity at large), you cannot see the point. Your strength certainly does lie with the material and the functional, but don't let that blind you to the possibility that there may be other dimensions in life. Just because you cannot, or have not, experienced something, does not mean that it cannot exist. If you can entertain the possibility that there may be more to existence than you imagine, you can lift your effectuality to something truly impressive.

Souls that have chosen a Life Path Four have a lesson to learn to live in harmony with restriction. In this lifetime, they have the opportunity to create something concrete in the physical universe. Often, the previous life has been excessively idealistic – the soul may have had ideas that didn't come to fruition. The purpose of Fours is to get the ideas out of their head and into the world. Being very solid and stable, it is possible that they may get stuck in unfulfilling relationships or jobs. They also have very fixed ideas and have a tendency to block input from others. This soul will make the most progress on this path if they can learn to be more open and less fixed. It takes courage to move on and embrace change, but sometimes it is the right thing to do.

Tips for Number Fours:

- Put 'relax', 'go out for a meal', 'go to the cinema' and other leisurely activities in your diary, and stick to those dates as rigidly as you do to work and duty commitments.

- Do something with your hands, such as model building, painting or pottery.

- At the end of each day, write down three things that have brought you joy.

LIFE PATH NUMBER FIVE

Souls that have chosen a Life Path Five have normally spent many, many lives being restricted in some way. They might have repeatedly chosen to take holy orders, hiding behind walls of an institution. In some way, the soul has lived many lives according to strict rules and regulations. By choosing a Five, the soul is ready to break down the mental and physical barriers that have prevented it from expressing the total freedom that is its birth right.

You are on a mission to become educated, and it is very important to you to feel you know a thing or two and are learning three or four more. If you don't have the opportunity to go to university, for instance, you will probably feel very discontent. Having said that, you always find a way to achieve your goals because you are resourceful and adaptable to the extreme.

You probably have several strings to your bow and it is quite possible that you can do more than one job. Your mind is quick and your knowledge of some subjects encyclopaedic, but you can also be deft with your hands.

Creativity is very important to you. Making something feels magic to you, and you are fascinated by the laws that govern the universe. You want to be able to work with these and manipulate them as much as possible. Once you have completed a task, you cannot wait to get on with the next one. Sometimes, you can be quite casual about what you achieve because once you understand something it seems easy. However, you love to show other people the way to do it because you are a great communicator. You are usually able to get on with people from all walks of life. You make a great teacher, journalist, writer and communicator. You love to travel and explore and experience other ways of living.

A Five, who is on track, will speak several languages, have more than one job, have friends of both sexes outside of marriage, have a home in two different countries, and will also enjoy various hobbies.

Being a jack-of-all-trades, whatever you do in life must produce variety and be constantly intriguing, otherwise you will not be at your best and you will feel frustrated. You could even become cranky and slightly mentally unstable if you have to conform to rigid timetables and repetitive work. In life, you are likely to experience many changes – in twenty years, you will likely be in a completely different place, externally and internally. Always communicate – people can cope with your changeability if they know what is going on.

Tips for Number Fives:

- Keep a journal – it is a way of capturing your wide life experience.

- Sign up for short-term classes, so you have things you can complete without running out of steam.

- Learn a foreign language; if you already speak one, learn another.

LIFE PATH NUMBER SIX

You want to make a difference in your community. As a child, you may have dreamed of being a doctor, nurse or teacher; an element of caring, healing and nurturing will be present in what you do.

It is not always easy for you to make a decision, and you need to feel that what you choose is supported by the group you are in. You call meetings and have discussions, easing everyone towards a consensus. You are good at seeing the bigger picture, and your approach is inclusive. This means that you are a terrific asset in situations that call for diplomacy and tact. You probably feel responsible for the comfort, well-being and success of everyone around you, and are committed and dedicated. However, sometimes you can spread yourself too thinly, trying too hard to be all things to all people.

Your love for peace means that you need to get away from it all when conflict arises. You are, however, a fabulous team player, often holding the side together, not so much through your inspired leadership, but through empathy. You have the ability to create a sense of family.

It's important to you to be surrounded by beauty and grace. Culture and art feature in your life, and you may well be artistic yourself. You encourage others to be creative and find themselves through play.

A soul on Life Path Six endeavours to bring beauty and love into the world. The nature of a Six is very giving – they want to create a better and more harmonious world. People who need help and support are instinctively drawn towards a Six. Very often, this soul has come directly from a life of violence and discord. It is not uncommon for the soul to have been killed in war in their last life. Sometimes, a soul will choose a Life Path Six if they have been responsible for the desecration of nature. They choose to redress the damage of their prior life by creating things of beauty in this life. Sixes have high standards and they seek perfection, leading to a state of dissatisfaction when these standards are not reached.

A Six, who is on track, will find themselves in situations of responsibility, giving help and comfort to others. They will have learned to discern between those who genuinely need their help and those who are 'users'. They will therefore only choose to support the weak and the vulnerable. They can be very successful in the arts.

Tips for Number Sixes:

- Invest in one or two original works of art, especially if you know the artist. Even the most modest budget will give you joy.

- Have a mini clear-out each week, even if it is only one cupboard or drawer – clutter is un-aesthetic.

- Find a good group to be a meaningful part of.

LIFE PATH NUMBER SEVEN

Number Seven is the contemplative truth seeker – they are here to seek spiritual truth. Those with a Life Path Seven have a sensitivity of the heart. These souls are choosing to re-balance their heart in this lifetime. In their previous life, their heart has likely been damaged in some way, either by being too hard-hearted or too soft-hearted. Having suffered the pain of a broken heart in the last life, the soul is seeking to re-build the structure of the heart. It could be that, having closed-off the heart as a means of coping with over-sensitivity, you over protected the heart by being too hard on others. This will have caused you great pain. The answer in this lifetime is to allow the heart centre to be opened.

By choosing Life Path Seven, the soul is being given the opportunity to build a balanced heart centre. Sceptical in nature, they are here to question the meaning of life. They are a good student and love to learn something that stimulates their mind. Those on this life path often choose to become spiritual as a way of balancing the heart. Unlike conditional human love, divine unconditional love never lets you down, and is therefore a safe way to open the heart to love.

The challenge for a Number Seven is that they can be secretive and untrusting until someone has earned their trust. It is not unusual for a Seven to choose to live alone and not be in a relationship at all. A Seven can be hard to get to know, keeping their feelings and emotions inside. Don't give up. They are just testing the waters to see who you really are. Once you've earned the trust of a Seven, they will be your friend for life. Other people are uplifted by the positive energy of a Seven.

It's important to note that Sevens need space and time alone. A Seven, who is on track, will be analysing the world in a quiet and calm way. They will be working from intuition and using their skills in the outer world by working as a teacher, counsellor or healer. They will not be focussed on the material benefits of their work, rather using their fine mind and powers of connection to the spiritual realms in the service of others. Some may even express the language of the heart through song and poetry. This is a life path to choose to explore the inner landscape. Without a connection to the heart and inner divinity, the life of a Seven will lack meaning.

Tips for Number Sevens:

- Spend regular time alone, ensuring that you enjoy your own company.

- Find something interesting to probe, such as your family tree.

- Do crosswords and puzzles regularly – they will keep your mind supple and distract you from negative thinking.

LIFE PATH NUMBER EIGHT

Number Eights are the business minded leaders. They have the ability to attract abundance into this life because Eight is the number of abundance (also lucky in Chinese). Not all are though. Some have a poverty consciousness. A person with a Life Path Eight must cultivate efficiency, business acumen, and an understanding of the laws governing the accumulation, power and use of money.

Eight is a powerful number with the law of attraction. Those with a Life Path Eight make good problem solvers, organisers and managers. Their main challenge is that they can be domineering and controlling. But, if you want something done and someone to run the ship, Eights should be in charge.

With Eight as your Life Path number, the will to power is strong within you. You have a relentless drive for material security, breadth of choice, and scope for effective action. You are probably very aware of the power struggles in the collective – big business, society at large, and closer to home. Instinctively, you will know who makes the decisions and why, and in any area that interests you, you will progress at a steady rate.

Status is vital to you, but try not to judge yourself and others by possessions. Driven and determined, you take yourself very seriously. Sometimes, others may find you overpowering, even though deep down you are very conscious of the potency of others, and often feel at a disadvantage. Being competitive and hierarchical, you have your eyes on the top job and are destined to be a tycoon. However, it may be better for you to be a big fish in a small pond, rather than head for the open sea, which may be shark-infested. In the end, you need to find a stronger power within you, and find spiritual meaning in what you do, so that your achievements can enrich you on all levels.

These souls are deep and powerful and can be quite a force to be reckoned with. The soul choosing to experience Life Path Eight will likely have encountered extreme excess or extreme deprivation in a previous life. This could be the soul that has starved to death through their inability to manifest the resources necessary to sustain life. It can also be the soul who has recently experienced a life of incredible abundance, taking far more than their fair share of the Earth's resources. During the reflection period between lives, the soul will have recognised the imbalance they experienced and will be seeking to address this by choosing the Life Path Eight.

An Eight, who is on track, will be in a position of responsibility. They have great organisational skills and loads of energy. They can become very wealthy and successful, but the lesson is to be satisfied with achieving material success, and then to open their heart to share their material resources with others. Once balanced, the Eight can enjoy the material universe and the comfort of nice things. Attaining money, status and power is not the final goal of an Eight. The goal is the satisfaction of becoming materially self-sufficient, and using their power in a compassionate and caring way.

Tips for Number Eights:

- Train yourself in business and finance. Pick a sensible course to study.

- Look closely at the life and philosophy of your favourite successful person and note what you can learn from them.

- Create a five-year game plan and review it regularly.

Life Path Nine

Number Nines are the compassionate humanitarians. They are the Gandhi's and the Mother Theresa's of the world. They often work in a career of service and education, in health or the government sector or social welfare, for example. Others are artistic and greatly gifted, or drawn to performing arts. Nines are very understanding and generous. They can, however, be intolerant and vengeful at times. So, one of their main life lessons is to learn forgiveness. Number Nines are who we need to make this world a better place.

With Nine as your Life Path number, what you perceive as truth is very important to you, so much so that the nature of 'truth' itself may be something you reflect on. You have the path of the teacher and philosopher. You know deep inside that you are 'meant' to do something for the collective, and so you may be working your way towards letting go of personal attachments. This stops you getting too tied to the mundane or the trivial. There will be times when you feel that you have to do things for the greater good of humanity and the planet.

You may feel drawn to making profound changes and even to becoming a spiritual leader. You may become absorbed by political, humanitarian, environmental and charity causes. You can be very selfless, but on the flip side, you may possess fanatical or dogmatic views. Liberty for all may be high on your agenda, but you may struggle to give 'liberty' to anyone that disagrees with you and your version of 'the truth'.

You can be very determined and possess a sense of mission that is galvanic. Because of your deep knowledge of human nature, you know how to motivate the collective. You may be good at getting publicity in the media or persuading famous and influential people to back your cause. You have a massive amount to offer the world. Anyone who has you on their side is blessed, as you put your heart and passionate belief behind them.

The soul who wants to turn over a new leaf will often choose to incarnate in Life Path Nine. This soul has come to the realisation that they are on a journey and, at some point, will need to return to Source. At a soul level, they have realised that they are a droplet from the ocean and that their destination is the ocean itself. We are all connected, all aspects of one consciousness. The soul of a Life Path Nine has chosen to move their soul towards acting upon this realisation. The main lesson of the Nine is to learn to give purely for the satisfaction of helping others, and not to be rewarded. This is how a spiritually advanced being acts, offering their life in service to others and giving selflessly.

During the reflection period between lives, this soul will have chosen to review all previous lifetimes. They will have identified a pattern of selfishness running like a thread throughout their lifetimes. Now, they are ready to deal with that aspect of themselves and open themselves up to the idea of losing their ego. They want to change, and are trying to do so by choosing Life Path Nine. To move away from selfishness, Nines need to learn to think of the needs and feelings of other people. In this lifetime, they are learning to give to others. They can find themselves placed in situations where they have little choice but to give, such as being a nursemaid to a sick child or carer to an elderly relative. The key lesson is to surrender to their situation and give with selfless love.

A Nine, who is on track, will be involved in charity work, caring for the sick, needy or under privileged. Their giving might be in the form of friendship or love towards others. They will be giving for the sake of giving and not for any reward or return. To help others selflessly requires practical work. Once on track and surrendered to giving, this Life Path brings huge reward at the level of the soul.

Tips for Number Nines:

- Find a worthwhile cause to champion – remember, you can always change this at a future date.

- Choose good, conscious-raising books, and always have one

by your bedside.

- Try to go abroad once a year to interact with people from other cultures.

LIFE PATH NUMBER ELEVEN

A soul that has chosen the Life Path Eleven has chosen to experience being in the physical universe while carrying a vibration that can be used for the good of others. The Eleven (a compound number) carries a much higher vibration than the single digits.

Eleven is the destiny of inspiration. Eleven is a master number in numerology, and it has a strong spiritual vibration. It is a number of high tension and great power. When it becomes too difficult to live with, you may revert to Two, which is not a master number and therefore easier to handle. With Eleven as your Life Path, you must investigate mysticism. Trust your intuition, have faith, live humbly in the limelight, and inspire others by your own example.

Two is the destiny of association with other people. In reverting back to this number, you must cultivate patience, diligence, cooperation, observation, tact, loyalty, and the ability to follow the lead of others.

As a Life Path Eleven, you are an inspirational teacher or spiritual messenger. You are still a Two, so a co-operative peace maker also, but there is something mystical about you. The Eleven has the ability to uplift, empower and inspire others, but you are also here on a very big journey of personal development. You will need to overcome a lot of your lower self to reach your full potential.

Challenges may be that you can be dishonest, manipulative, lack self-confidence, and need to work on loving and believing in yourself. On the plus side, you are outgoing, magnetic, charismatic and loving.

Your life purpose is to uplift, empower and inspire those that cross your path. Your soul, through your actions in previous incarnations, has decided that it is ready to take its place on Earth and be of use in some way. However, it may be that you are living a perfectly ordinary life – bringing this elevated vibration into the earth plane of physical reality is not quite as easy as it might have appeared from the astral plane.

When we are on the astral plane, there is a lightness of being. Time isn't like it is here on Earth. Grandiose plans that appear perfectly possible to manifest from that level of consciousness are suddenly experienced as very difficult here on the earth plane. It's a bit like the difference between walking through air and walking through mud. Things are much slower, heavier, and more cumbersome here on Earth.

The soul on Life Path Eleven is charged with energy. This energy is held within the nervous system. Too much of this energy buzzing through them can cause the Eleven to be very highly strung.

Tips for Number Elevens:

- Listen to your inner voice to find your mission.

- Remember, truth has many faces, and your truth might not match everyone else's.

- Search within yourself for a special talent.

[Full Personal Numerology reports are available through the Angelic Energies website: www.AngelicEnergies.co.uk]

SOUL PURPOSE

As well as a life purpose, you also have a soul purpose. I'll explain the difference. Your soul purpose is energy based and is really very simple – to express and experience divinity; to identify with every living being on the planet and in the cosmos; to become an expression of pure unconditional love in every aspect of your life; and to understand that the entire universe is an expression in physical form of the divinity itself.

We come into this world forgetting who we really are. This is the toughest training ground because we, as humans, are the only beings that forget that we are extensions of Source consciousness. We have this illusion of separation, and we experience the limiting 3D reality of lack, quite often believing that we are not enough. Difficult circumstances have us believe that we need to struggle, that we can't have what we want, that life is unfair.

It's not until we transform our thinking - fully letting go of our limiting beliefs and awakening to the fact that we are pure potential standing here on the cutting edge of creation - that we can begin to live the life that we were born to. We are unlimited beings capable of anything that we set our minds to. Our soul purpose is to wake up to the reality of our own personal power. Divinity is not something outside of us; it is the very fibre of our being, along with everything else in existence.

Your life purpose is more action based. It's what your soul has decided to experience in this lifetime to expand and grow. It's not always linked to what you do for a living. It can simply be a reflection of your attitude and beliefs. Our purpose should be thought of as a process, rather than a goal. This can evolve over many lifetimes. One clue is to look at where your talents and skills lie. These gifts are an intricate part of your purpose.

Ask yourself, what do you feel passionate about that you feel could make a difference in the world? You need to follow your heart with vision and actions. Allow yourself quiet time, away from all gadgets and gizmos, to connect with yourself and the divine, and embrace the awareness of your soul. Spend 15 - 20 minutes each day in meditation, connecting on a different level with cosmic awareness and reality. This will bring you in line with your mind, body and soul.

Our life purpose depends on our individual make-up of what makes us unique. As we have seen, Numerology (as well as Astrology) provides wonderful insight into our hidden depths. The more we learn about ourselves, the more we can appreciate the deeper understanding of what makes us special, and the greater harmony we can experience as a result.

I imagine that, at the end of each lifetime, our soul goes into counsel with highly developed beings to review our expansion. From there it is decided what our soul should go on to undertake in the next lifetime. From a non-physical perspective, challenges seem easy as there is no resistance. It's not until we incarnate back into physical reality that we're subjected to the harsh reality of this world. As we are born into a world of duality and contrast, in order to discover what we want, we first have to experience the lack of it. The most advanced souls are often born into the most challenging circumstances. I believe that we pick our family in accordance with how we want to develop. They are our soul group that have agreed to facilitate our development, for better or worse. It's up to us to heal from these challenges, and use this to transform into a drive for something better for humanity.

Master Morya (or El Morya) who helped found the Theosophical Society, states that, if you want to know the destiny of your soul, look at the trend of your thinking. Become self-aware enough to look at your natural instinct of interest and enquiry. There is a golden thread in that trend. Ask yourself, what do you like to think about? Not the day to day thoughts, but rather the bigger picture. Are you, for example, more science based, or alternative healing? Follow the trend of your thinking that leads to bliss.

I don't actually think there's a wrong or right way to live. There's nothing we specifically need to achieve. Naturally, we always want more, and this pushes us further to achieve. However, we can become so consumed with the 'doing' that we forget to enjoy just 'being'. I believe that the world around us is an illusion. Reality is subjective – we all experience things differently. As the saying goes, 'One man's hell is another man's paradise.' The most important thing to focus on is to live from the heart space. In every action we take, we have a choice. We can either come from a place of fear, or of love. Life is that simple. It's up to us to consciously choose to come from a place of pure unconditional love, knowing that this is our true essence. When we align with that, everything flows our way. When we witness otherwise, send compassion. By following what lights us up, what gives us joy, we're being who we are meant to be. The world needs more people who are lit up, to inspire others to shine their own light. You were born to be happy, fulfilled and full of grace. You are a divine being, capable of anything you set your mind to.

Our soul is inherent goodness. It is the eternal aspect to our being, one that allows us to feel loved and to experience that we are love. Angels are so special because they are thoughts that lift us from the limiting cages that our ego tries to contain us in. Angels are the bridge to connect us to our true eternal state of bliss and pure unconditional love. When we live through the heart, we are in line with our soul purpose.

Simply put, our purpose in this lifetime is to experience joy. If you had one goal on this planet, that would be it. This is the only true motivation for anything. Everything we do is done so because we think it will make us feel better. We ultimately understand that joy is our purpose. The challenge is to actively choose thoughts and actions that make us feel good. If we made it a priority to align with joy, then there would be no horrendous crimes. By following our passion and what lights us up, our purpose will automatically find us. We are a physical incarnation of our Source self, and the feelings of passion allow us to know when we are aligned with Source. Evolution, in general, is the by-product of following joy.

While growing up, we're typically taught to care about what other people think, rather than to live in alignment with what feels good for us. We then go on to lose track of where we're going, and life becomes one of great effort. As a by-product of this, if the carers we had while growing up continually put their own needs before us as a child, we are likely to get into the cycle of expecting others to suffer in order to prove their love for us. Humans are the only beings in existence that defer getting our needs met. If an animal is hungry, it will go out and get food. It won't question it's worthiness as to whether it deserves food.

Finding our purpose is a matter of taking the risk of caring how we feel, and following what feels good. This could mean letting go of things that you've invested a lot of time and effort into, but if you're not living in alignment with what feels good, you don't have enough energy to be able to stay in a place of health.

We didn't come to Earth to play it safe in accordance with everyone else's wishes. Our purpose isn't going to express itself in what we're going to get and achieve. It's going to express itself in what gifts we have to give to this world. Your purpose will always be to ask yourself how you can express yourself. So, to discover your purpose, follow your joy, and ask yourself what is trying to express through you today.

Archangel Michael can help us when we become fearful. He can help us feel safe and protected. When we get scared, a physiological response is initiated and the fight-or-flight response kicks in. Our digestive system shuts down, and our body focuses its energy on producing cortisol and adrenaline, which are designed to get us up and out of the way of danger. This was beneficial in ancient times when sabre-toothed tigers threatened our survival, but serves little purpose in our daily lives now. However, our brains are still hardwired to default to looking for problems and seeing the negative in situations.

We do, however, live in a world ruled by the law of attraction, so whatever we think and feel is reflected in the world around us. Training ourselves to always look for the good in everyone and every situation is the most beneficial thing we can do for ourselves. On a conscious level, we don't get to choose what happens to us, but as we reach adulthood, we do get to choose how we respond. Take what has occurred and use it to awaken - rather than perpetuate - the cycle of pain. Everything we experience can be viewed as a lesson; provided we learn the lesson, we need not experience it again. There are life situations that you cannot change, but you can always choose how you respond, and in that, you will find your freedom.

People need to take responsibility for their actions and not use their power to hurt and harm others. There is no separation; only oneness. We are all awakening to the truth that love is the only real thing.

If you are in a state of fear, face it head-on and recognise this as your truth. Then, begin to question whether or not your fear is real. Love is big, bold, powerful, and compassionate. We are currently living a dream that is designed to awaken our unlimited God consciousness. We are the creators of our own reality.

What you believe is true. Self-doubt is paralysing. It contributes towards people choosing misery over joy, emptiness over fulfilment, imprisonment over freedom, and unnecessarily so. Believe in yourself. Regaining your ability to believe in yourself gives you the power to change the direction of your life. Your past does not have to define your future. You have a choice whether to let the past define or refine you. You don't have to wait for a miracle. You can create your own.

PERSONAL POWER AND SOUL PURPOSE MEDITATION

I now invite you to get comfortable and take some long, deep breaths, all the way down into your belly. We're going to start by dedicating a few precious moments to just being with our breath. Feel your chest rise up as you inhale fully. Breathe right down to the bottom of your lungs. Then, relax. Allow all the stale air that you no longer need to leave your body. Now, take a big, full deep inhale. Fill those lungs to maximum capacity, then simply release. Continue taking those big, deep, life affirming breaths, letting go of all the tension, all the stress, as you arrive fully present in the moment. Feel how your body feels the gratitude as you receive the extra oxygen you need to support your wellbeing.

We call upon Archangel Michael to be with us now. We ask that his courageous energy and strength support us as he assists us in finding our personal power, our soul's purpose.

We now make a conscious choice to take back all the power that we have given away. We invite all of the energy that we have given away to be brought back to us in this moment. All the power that we have handed over to others, we ask to be brought back to us in the moment, and that it is washed clear with the love light of Source.

Breathing all of that new energy that belongs to you back into your body. As you're breathing into your body, you're filling it up with the loving light of our own soul's essence. Now place all of your focus on the soles of your feet. We now allow ourselves to open up and be nourished by the energy of Mother Earth. This energy is always available to us, to ground us and support our wellbeing. We intend that the portholes in our feet chakras are now opening up. You might like to picture a bright teal blue light flowing down your legs and through the centre of your feet. You are opening this energy centre and allowing energy to balance and neutralise into the earth. Take a moment to feel this wonderful nurturing connection with the earth as it supports you in all that you do.

You are experiencing oneness with this life force energy. We now invite this energy to move up into our solar plexus, the area above our navel and in our belly and chest. Take another big deep life affirming breath in as we renew our sense of power in our own body, our own self. We're commanding the clearing out of any feelings of disempowerment, loneliness, the energy of being too small to make a difference in this world, all these feeling of powerlessness. Fear is false evidence appearing real. We're clearing this out of our energy body.

Just breathe. Allow this wonderful expanded energy to work for you. Relax and allow the energy to move through your body. Now, we are downloading Source's true perspective of empowerment that each body and soul is unlimited in its potential. Hold that incredible freedom in to your body for a moment.

We understand that we exist in one collective consciousness. When you are present, the infinite potential that is present within the field of one is available to you. When you are present you are able to empower positive change in the world by simply being, by tuning into your intuition and following inspired action in the present moment with your heart open. Breathing, being aware and living in your power. The infinite possibility to transform your life is available. The infinite possibility to transform the world is available. From this place of being aware, breathing, being present, being aware of the love which surrounds you and letting that be your main focus, you are able to manifest your intentions and your heart's desires.

From this place of soul connection, ask yourself now, 'What is in your heart's desire to manifest? What is your heart calling for you to move into as the doors of infinite possibility open before you now?' Breathe, become aware of your intention of your soul, your higher spirit.

All the guidance and reassurance we need is available to us now. Just take a moment to connect with the stillness and ask yourself, 'What is my soul purpose?' Relax and take whatever comes to you in whatever form it may appear. Switch on all your senses so that you may feel, hear, see or know the guidance coming to you now. Ask yourself, 'What is my soul purpose?' What do you want to create, to fully embody and receive? Open your heart and become aware of this knowing now.

Your heart is the sacred porthole to the higher realms. So, with this new download, allow yourself to feel the emotions of this manifested into reality. As you align with your soul's desire, feel how this resonates throughout your body. Feel your energy expanding and elevating as you embrace your truth or your internal calling. You are one with all that is, and fully connected with the Universe.

With this new integration of the cosmic truth of our power, we become a sovereign responsible steward of our reality. We understand that we create our own reality with our consciousness, and so the most empowering thing we can do for our world right now is to clear out all the distortions. Embrace your infinite power as a divine spark of the one universal energy. You are love, the highest vibration, and you are here to light up the world.

As we are closing, I'm going to pull in blankets of golden light energy to cover your body with the intention that, all of the shifts that were made today that resonate with your highest love, highest truth and highest joy, be permanent. We give thanks to Archangel Michael for his guidance and support, and to the earth for sustaining our energy. We ask that the love and joy that we have embodied be shared with the earth for the highest good of all. And so it is.

AFFIRMATIONS FOR ARCHANGEL MICHAEL

'Thank you, Archangel Michael, for ensuring that I am a very successful person.'

'Thank you, Archangel Michael, for making sure that I can tackle anything that life throws at me.'

'Thank you, Archangel Michael, for helping me to every day take steps towards achieving my goals.'

'Thank you, Archangel Michael, for protecting me and my loved ones. I understand that love is always the greatest and most powerful energy of protection.'

The scented healing mist from Angelic Energies for Archangel Michael is dedicated solely to incense. This is a pure blend of myrrh and frankincense, balanced softly with woods. Incense is a sacred tool used for thousands of years, and the classic harmony of natural resins creates a spiritual harmony.

You are invited to indulge your senses and feel a deep connection with the Divine with the exquisite Scented Healing Mists from Angelic Energies. Attuned to the Archangels and charged with Angelic Reiki, these are a beautiful way to build your spiritual practise through cleaning your aura and raising your vibration. Available at www.AngelicEnergies.co.uk.

Chapter 5:
Archangel Raphael

Healing and Safe Travel

Super Powers   Boost Healing / Reduce Cravings and Addictions / Rejuvenation /Vitality / Safe Journey

Name Translation   God Heals

Crystal   Emerald, Malachite, Green Aventurine

Colour   Emerald green

Helping People   Travelling long distance or flying, pain control, addictions and craving reduction, healing.

Ray   5th Green Ray of healing

Archangel Raphael, meaning 'God Heals', comes in on the 5th green ray of healing and prosperity. His story comes from the book of Tobit. Archangel Raphael appeared as a human being, travelling with a crowd who were moving from one part of the holy land to another. This is how he become known as the patron of travellers. He is said to have helped a man at the side of the road regain his sight. This lead him to be recognised as the Healing Angel.

Archangel Raphael has an emerald green light that can improve all aspects of injury and illness, including reduction of addictions and cravings. He also assists healers in their healing practice, giving them a thought, idea or message to take positive action.

He is known to carry a healing staff known as a caduceus. This snake entwined staff with surmounted wings is seen on the side of ambulances. It was also carried by Hermes, in Greek mythology, Mercury, in Roman mythology, and Iris, the messenger of Hera, in Egyptian mythology. As mentioned, Archangel Raphael is also known as the guardian of travellers. You can call upon him while flying or driving long distances to ensure a safe and harmonious journey.

When wanting to make a change in lifestyle, e.g. cutting something out of your diet or exercising more, it helps to have the correct focus. Let's say you want to lose weight, for example. By telling yourself that you can't have that biscuit or chocolate bar, you're only going to want it more – far better to keep reminding yourself of what you stand to gain, rather than what you have to lose. Tell yourself, every day, that you are getting slimmer. Love your body and be grateful for it as it is now. Imagine yourself fitting into the clothes that you want. Keep your focus on what you want, rather than what you don't yet have.

If you are struggling with your health, do not allow fear to take over.

Stay focused on imagining yourself being free of pain, or if this is not possible, stay firmly in the present moment. As difficult as it may be, try not to resist the pain, and instead sink into it and be fully present with it.

Ask your body what it is wanting you to know by bringing up this pain. Trust that the sensation of the pain is an indicator that, on a cellular level, your body is working hard to repair itself. By resisting the pain, you are only putting up barriers to repair.

Remember, you are not your illness. Don't let it become your identity. One of the most inspirational people to have overcome cancer is Anita Moorjani, who credited her illness to a lack of self-love, and the focus on fear and worry. She defied all odds, and spectacularly came back from the brink of death to transform her life. Anita is now a beacon spreading the truth that Heaven is not a destination; it's a state of being. I highly recommend reading her books 'Dying to be Me' and 'What if this is Heaven?'

THE POWER OF THE BREATH

There are many things we can do to support our wellbeing. One of the most important is to breathe correctly. Most of the time, we breathe at only 20-30% of our capacity. The more we can oxygenate our body, the less we feel stressed, as our nervous system stabilises. We also experience more energy and alertness. When the body gets enough oxygen, the immune system is improved as well. Low levels of oxygen in the body can lead to severe medical conditions, so consciously breathing can transform your life in more ways than one.

'Improper breathing is a common cause of ill health. If I had to limit my advice on healthier living to just one tip, it would simply be to learn how to breathe correctly. There is no single more powerful - or more simple - daily practise to further your health and wellbeing than breath work.' - Andrew Wil, M.D.

Oxygen is the source of all energy in the body and drives our metabolic processes. Yogis call it Prana, or life force energy. Interestingly, the most common killer of cells in our body is lack of oxygen. Furthermore, a study on rats by Dr Harry Goldblatt showed that those with under-oxygenated cells developed cancer.

We can go three weeks without food, two or three days without water, but only a few minutes without breathing. The more oxygen we have, the higher the quality of life we have in a physical, mental and spiritual capacity.

Breath work is the most efficient and effective way to overcome ourselves. 95% of our daily thoughts and actions happen on autopilot. Breathing exercises help us to take control of our lives by reminding us to be fully present, allowing us to choose to align with our authentic integrity and highest self.

If you live in either the past or the future, you can feel depressed, stressed, anxious or embarrassed. Focused attention on the breath brings you into the present moment where you feel naturally complete, confident, and in the flow of life. Conscious breathing enables you to control your thoughts, which in turn controls your emotions, which control your actions, which control your habits, and so your entire life.

Stand now and take a deep breath. Most probably, your chest will come out, your head and shoulders will go back, and your stomach is pulled in. Breathing like this is only using 50 - 70% of your total capacity. When most of us take a deep breath, we push the diaphragm up and pull the stomach in, collapsing the bottom half of our lungs in the process.

The correct way to breathe is from the belly; nice deep breaths so the belly comes out.

Deep breathing allows for deep thinking.

Take a moment now to be aware of your breathing. Is it rhythmic or hectic? Shallow or deep? Abdominal or in the chest? Many of us hold our breath without realising. Try a simple breathing meditation now. Keep the breath normal as you count to four on the inhale, pause for a moment, then count to four on the exhale. Thoughts will appear; don't attach to them and let them pass by. Bring your focus back to the breath and keep counting.

If you are feeling depressed, in a bad mood, stressed, anxious, or about to have a panic attack, do Bhastrika breathing. Take a forceful breath in and stretch your hands up in the air with open hands and fingers. Fill up your lungs fully, then pause for a moment. Then, exhale forcefully, snapping your arms back, while pulling your hands to your shoulders and clenching your fists and face as forcefully as you can, then releasing. Repeat this cycle ten times. This is also a great way to start the day and get your energy flowing.

There are many other breathing techniques you can try. Another example is to do three full inhales through the mouth to the fullest capacity, keeping your body relaxed and breath connected, not pausing. Sit back, and notice that breathing through your mouth allows a faster pace to get more oxygen quickly, and on the exhale, relax and let it go. Commit to five minutes (or 100 breaths) every day. This will bring balance into your life. Do this for an hour and things will profoundly shift. Make sure you do this sitting down as you may get dizzy; the body is not accustomed to working at this level of oxygenation.

In general, aim to get into the habit of deeper, fuller, relaxed breathing to keep the body in an optimum state. As mentioned, breathe from the belly, pushing it out as you fill the lower levels of the lungs up. Watch the mind become clearer as a result.

When implementing a new habit into your life, you must link it with an existing automatic action that you already have. Decide that the same automatic behaviour will trigger your breathing exercise.

Incorporate breath meditation into your everyday activities, such as when you're heading to the train station in the morning. As you're walking along, be aware of your breath – breathing in for three strides and out for four. Every time your attention wanders, bring it back to your breath.

Personally, I find it highly beneficial to do deep conscious breathing while driving. I have noticed that, quite often when driving, I tend to hold my breath as I concentrate. This is, of course, very bad for the body and increases stress levels. So, as soon as I become aware of this, I switch to a few rounds of deep breathing. Whenever you schedule your breathing exercises, it's also a good idea to drink water.

Make the decision now to commit to harnessing the power of the breath.

MORE WAYS TO BOOST YOUR WELLBEING

Another life-affirming action you can do is to take Omega 3, 6 & 9 as well as Q10 capsules daily, along with a good quality vitamin and mineral supplement. Even if we think we eat a healthy diet, taking these vitamin supplements is the fastest way to boost mitochondrial function. These are tiny bacteria that live in nearly every cell in our body, and are responsible for creating energy. The number, efficiency and strength of your mitochondria dictate whether or not you'll develop cancer or a degenerative disease, so it pays to keep them in peak condition. Omega oils are healthy fats that are vital for healthy brain function and to feel sharp, focused, effective, reliable, and with a constant stream of energy. The brain is nearly 70% fat and needs this to run as fuel to stop it from shrinking.

Being in poor quality (fluorescent) light drains us. Try to get some infrared and ultraviolet rays, present in daylight. Too much sugar increases the amount of insulin in the blood, which damages organs within the body, so try to stabilise blood sugar levels. Food manufacturers load products with sugar to get it to the 'bliss point' so that we get addicted to it. We carry on eating processed food because our body does not recognise that it is satisfied, as it doesn't provide the nutrients we require. Even worse, this sugar is artificial. The effect of artificial sugar on the body is reportedly worse than heroin. Our brain is literally lit up like a pinball machine because of it. Diet sodas and most children's drinks contain this artificial sugar which you can see on the label as Acesulfame K (containing the carcinogen methylene chloride), and aspartame (also known as E951). Upon ingestion, aspartame breaks down into components (aspartic acid, phenylalanine and methanol) then further products including formaldehyde and formic acid, known to be toxic. Reports of reactions to aspartame have included headaches, migraines, premature birth, cancer, seizures, depression, ADHD and MS. Interestingly, the NHS advises pregnant women to avoid aspartame and artificial sweeteners. Processed food, simple carbohydrates, such as white flour and white rice, margarine and dairy are also to be avoided to ensure optimal health.

Make a conscious effort to drink filtered water. Most of us exist in a state of dehydration. Realise if you're feeling thirsty, you are already very dehydrated. Have a glass of water with you at all times, and take regular sips throughout the day. Notice your skin improving and your eyes sparkling as your appetite reduces and your figure improves.

Water is the closest vibrational match to source energy, which is why we feel rejuvenated when we have a shower or bath. Try doing a shower meditation. Every time you take a shower, visualise washing away your stress and anxiety. Concentrate on the feeling of the water upon your skin. Envision the power of the water washing away your negative thoughts. Feel sadness, regret, anger and depression wash right off you. Let it all go down the drain. Feel lightness in your body. Enjoy the clarity of your mind. Your soul is free of all that does not serve your highest good. You are ready for a new beginning.

Grounding is another essential factor to live a healthy life. We are electromagnetic beings, and when we don't ground ourselves, we circulate the same energy, round and round. Nature is a wonderful stabiliser that regenerates us. It automatically attunes our biomagnetic field to what it should be. Being out in nature every single day is highly recommended for wellbeing. Grounding is also achieved through visualisation. Imagine silver roots, like the roots of the tree, sinking deep down into the earth until they reach a large crystal at the centre of Earth. Wrap those roots around that crystal and feel that connection to the earth. It is also highly beneficial to take your shoes and socks off and walk around feeling the earth directly. Grounding is also highly beneficial in combatting jet leg.

Seven Secrets of Self-Healing - How to Heal Yourself

No 1 - Believe. Believe that you can heal. Yes, you will hear all kinds of stories about people who have not recovered or people who are ill. It's about you. It's about your life and your life experience. There are millions of people who heal every day from the worse kinds of conditions. They heal because healing is possible. There are many incredible stories from Joe Dispenza about those that have followed his daily healing meditation, for example. If it's possible, it can happen to you. Stay away from stories about other people's illnesses, other people's conditions. It's about you. Believe and have faith that healing is possible.

No 2 - Remember, your thoughts create your reality. Your thoughts of illness create illness. Thoughts of health create health. Understand that your thoughts become things. They are magnetic;

they attract into your life the experiences of your life. Set the intention to think thoughts of health. Use affirmations to help you. This will keep all the negative, self-destructive thoughts away, and you will manifest health because this is your focus.

No 3 - Listen to your body. Listen to cravings. Your body will tell you if it needs nutrients. Or, it may communicate emotional needs, such as taking time out to watch a funny film. Your body will give you special signals as it's clearing and healing itself. So, listen. Pay attention to these subtle signals. Give the body what it needs for healing.

No 4 - Protect your energy. Don't seek advice or share your pain or emotions with people who take away your energy. You know who they are. Right now, you need energy for healing. You need to provide the right environment for healing to happen. It's crucial when you are self-healing to stay away from people who drain you or push your emotional buttons.

No 5 - Forgiveness. If you are holding onto pain from the past, that pain is like a parasite. It's taking up space and energy. It's destroying your energy and tissues from the inside. It's heavy, and it's real. When you process these emotions, when you let go, when you forgive, the pain begins to disintegrate. There's no food for that pain. When you're not energising the pain from the past with your thoughts, you are letting go. You are forgiving. You are processing all of your previous experiences, including forgiving yourself.

No 6 - Transcendence. This means going back to the original source from where you came, from where everything came. You do this through meditation, calming down, and being in nature. Silence is the place of miracles and possibility because you connect to source; the source that created the entire universe; the source that created you and your body. When you shift to a place of silence and transcendence, you heal. The longer you spend in that space, the faster your healing will happen.

No 7 - Visualise yourself as being healthy. Negative thoughts of fear may tempt you, but set the intention to see yourself healthy. Wake up and see yourself full of energy. Visualise your body being active and full of energy – beautiful, strong and confident. Do this consciously. You are not at the mercy of your circumstances. You are a conscious creator of your life and health. Do a five or 10-minute visualisation in the morning when your mind is quiet and receptive. See yourself healthy, joyful, laughing with your friends and family, and doing all the things that you want to do. Stay in that vibration; a self-healing mechanism will happen in your body, and healing will take place.

AFFIRMATIONS FOR ARCHANGEL RAPHAEL

'Thank you, Archangel Raphael, for helping me to have a strong, healthy body.'

'Thank you, Archangel Raphael, for ensuring that I am full of vitality and vigour.'

'Thank you, Archangel Raphael, for allowing me to travel safely knowing all my needs will be met.'

'Thank you, Archangel Raphael, for helping me get the best healer for my condition and get seen straight away.'

The Scented Healing Mist for Archangel Raphael is focused on comfort and healing. Incense is an ancient healing and connective power. Based in the rich resin of myrrh, it's paired with cedar, grounding and rooting it to the earth, and natural lavender essential oil.

CHAPTER 6:
ARCHANGEL GABRIEL

Children, Clear Speaking and Creativity

Super Powers   Inspiration in Creative Ideas / Courage and Opportunities for Expression / Communication / Public Speaking / Writing / Parenting / Performing Arts / Artists

Name Translation   The Strength of God

Crystal   Moonstone, Aquamarine, Pearls, Selenite

Colour   Silver, white, pale blue

Helping People   Expectant and adoptive parents. Those involved with new born projects. Fertility, childbirth and parenting. All those who work with self-expression, such as artists, writers, journalists, actors, singers, performers, and public speakers.

Ray   4th White Ray, representing harmony and purity

All Angels are androgynous, but you may associate Archangel Gabriel with being either female or male. Gabriel is said to be the Angel of revelation because God chose Gabriel to communicate important messages. She supports all those who wish to express themselves in every way, from acting and public speaking to writers, singers and artists .

Archangel Gabriel comes in on the 4th ray, which is white light, tinged with pink. This ray represents sensitivity, purity and truth. She came to Mother Mary to tell her that she was going to conceive and be the mother of Jesus. Archangel Gabriel also announced the birth of John the Baptist. As she is the Angel of Annunciation, she is associated with mothers, children and childbirth, and all aspects of parenting, including pregnancy and adoption.

Archangel Gabriel is known as the messenger Angel, and her name means 'The Strength of God'. She supports us in speaking our truth with integrity, and is excellent at helping us to push past procrastination so we can get things done. She guides and supports expectant and adoptive parents, as well as those involved in 'new born' creative projects.

HELP WITH CHILDREN

Becoming a parent is harder than anyone could imagine. It is, of course, the most worthwhile and the biggest lesson in love possible. Even the strongest person is tested by the sleep deprivation and sheer responsibility of being a parent. While there is no such thing as the perfect parent, one of the biggest things we can do is to realise the mistakes our own parents made, and break this pattern.

A child should be seen as an individual Divine creator, just as we are ourselves, and as parents, we should be their partner and their guide. A child has their own free will, and should not be seen or treated as a commodity. Our happiness should not be dependent upon them, or anyone else for that matter. Think back to the time when you were a child. What kind of parents do you wish you had? The two most important factors to remember when raising a child are to help them to gain emotional intelligence, and to have them understand consequences.

Punishment will never get good results. It is not energetically possible for something positive to come out of something negative. As parents, we have to find a way of controlling our anger and frustrations and not let this spill over to the child. Shouting and screaming at a child is not healthy for anyone. Remember to breathe and remind yourself that the child is having a hard time coping, and it's up to us as adults to help them through those moments. Unconditional love is about being with someone while they're having a hard time, as well as when things are going well. To be the best parent, we have to be unconditionally fully present with them, no matter how they feel.

Disciplining a child will not make them listen to you. It only serves to cause resentment. This will likely cause them to act out even further in later life, just to rebel against you. When you have a friendship with your child, there is room for correction. Let them see you as a human being too, and be honest with them and admit when you have made a mistake. If you're not being a good friend, they're not seeking your advice. They will get their answers online instead. By being a friend, you will naturally be able to influence them. Of course, they should understand the difference between right and wrong, but in a way that they can comprehend the consequences of their actions.

Criticising a child doesn't stop them loving you, it stops them loving themselves. When a child does something you disagree with, instead of condemning them, try and get them to see how their actions affect others. In doing so, you'll be helping to raise a compassionate human being who thinks of others and the impact they have on this world. Criticising them and getting them to feel bad about themselves causes them to reject that part of themselves. This splintering of consciousness leads to feelings of unworthiness as an adult where they no longer get their needs met. Every parent wants their child to grow up to be happy, yet they don't realise the damage they do in seemingly trying to do the best for their child. It's vital to stop and think about the long term effects your behaviour has on them.

Emotional intelligence is fostered by acknowledging and validating emotions. Many parents use the art of distraction to relieve an emotionally charged situation. Some are even disapproving of displays of emotion. The problem here is that, if a child is taught to dissociate from their emotions, they will abandon themselves. They will begin to feel isolated in the world, unable to connect with anyone around them. When this happens, they are setting themselves up for painful and destructive relationships in later life.

It's important to realise that every emotion a child feels is valid. Try and remember that they have only recently come from a place of unconditional love and abundance. To come into this world and be restricted by their parents' lack of abundance mentality and undemonstrative love is hard for them to cope with.

Express empathy and let them know that you understand how they are feeling, and that they have every right to feel that way. Perhaps add that, if you were them, you would feel the same. Once how they feel has been acknowledged, you can then start to help them move through the pain and offer suggestions on what they can do to help themselves. By validating the child's emotions, they don't need to hold on to their pain, or store it for trauma to emerge later in life.

When a child is playing up, the worst form of punishment is isolation. A popular way to deal with children who are acting out is to put them on the 'naughty step' or have 'time out', where they are left alone to consider their actions. This is done out of sheer exasperation of the parent, and it does nothing to help the child; in fact, it only makes them feel ten times worse. Instead of reflecting on how their actions have been inappropriate, the child will merely sit there raging about how unfair the situation is or how unloved they are. A better way is to have 'time in'. Ask the child to take a break and come and sit with you as you strengthen your connection with them, letting them know that you support them. We are all connected beings, and feeling otherwise threatens our very sense of survival.

We need to understand the emotions behind the actions. Ask the child why they did what they did, and get them to consider how that made the other person feel. We need to be cultivating compassionate human beings, not ones that feel isolated and unable to process their emotions. Problem solving is a fantastic way to solve conflict. Ask the child if they can come up with an idea to put the situation right. If they have hurt someone else's feelings, how can they make them feel better? This is a great skill to learn in preparation for adulthood.

For a child to grow up to be a responsible adult, they must be mindful of the consequences of their actions. Allow the child to make mistakes while they are young, as difficult as it may be to watch. This will hopefully prevent them from making big mistakes when they get older. Encourage them to think through their actions. Instead of simply saying no, explain why. Give them choices within the parameters of what is acceptable and possible at the time. Would they prefer to leave the park in one minute or three minutes? This way, it does not deteriorate to a battle of wills as they still have a sense of power and control.

Emotional intelligence can be developed by not trying to repress or dismiss the emotions of a child. As uncomfortable as we may feel, it's important to sit with them and allow them to feel their own emotions. Perhaps ask them where in their body they feel a particular emotion they are experiencing. Once their feelings have been fully acknowledged, then it is possible to empathise and suggest an alternative way of thinking about things.

Take a moment to think about what you would wish for your child once they have grown up. The chances are that the main priority is for them to be happy. This can only happen if they're confident and comfortable in their own body and mind, sure of who they are and what they are capable of. The only way this can be developed is when they are allowed to do things for themselves. By coming to their rescue all the time, we do not give them a chance to develop and learn. We need to empower our children, not perpetuate dependency.

Perhaps the child would like a toy, and you don't have the money to buy it for them. Rather than simply saying no, try explaining to them that you are not in a position to be able to buy it for them, and help them think up other ways that they can get it themselves. Let them see that you are not perfect. If you don't know the answer to something, admit it, and show them how they can find out for themselves. Every time we say no to a child, it kills off the neurotransmitters in their brain. The world needs people who can come up with solutions to problems, so foster this approach.

Children go through key stages in their lives, and it helps to be aware of these. Up until the age of six, a child's brain is in Theta state. This is the same open receptacle state as in meditation, so the child has no filters, and information just flows in without selection. Here they form the blueprint for their personality based on the environment around them. They are literally like sponges, soaking up our mannerisms and actions.

The next crucial stage is around 10 and 11. Here they learn how to break away energetically from the parent. There is focused attention on meeting their energetic needs, and helping them to establish their own energetic and personal boundaries.

The best thing you can do for your children is to be joyful. They absorb your emotions. If you are stressing out trying to give them everything, this is counter-productive. Encourage them to find their own joy so that they can shine their light out into the world. Let them know that all anyone wants is to feel their joy.

BULLYING

A dear friend of mine, Samantha, works in a secondary school in a fairly challenging area of the UK. She had been subjected to bullying by a group of pupils who had ganged up on her in the dinner hall, after she reprimanded one of their fellow classmates. From the children's perspective, they were trying to stick up for their friend in an effort to show they cared about that child. However, their threatening, malicious behaviour deeply affected Samantha, and she walked out of the school and was off sick as a result. She wasn't the only one; many of the staff were off work with stress.

I wanted Samantha to gain a different perspective on what was going on. The situation actually had nothing to do with her. In the children's eyes, she was just another person who was against them. These children came from care homes and broken homes, and felt very little sense of love and connection. Their low sense of self-esteem meant that the only way they could feel better about themselves was to make others feel worse. Their misguided behaviour was their way of showing their friend that they loved and cared for them.

I urged Samantha to try and see these children through the eyes of love, and recognise the pain that they were feeling inside and to validate that for them. In showing compassion, all barriers fall away. By assuring the children that she had their best interest in mind, she could help them recognise their own self-worth. Living in fear is no way to be. Remind the children that boundaries are there to help them develop into responsible adults. Encourage them to think about the impact their behaviour has on others. These children are our future. We need to be raising compassionate human beings, and the best way is to lead by example.

CREATIVITY AND COMMUNICATION

Archangel Gabriel can also give support in creative ventures. Those of us with more right-brain activity tend to be more artistic and creative, thoughtful and subjective. They perceive the world in a very visual way, relying on feelings and intuition. Those with a left-brain focus tend to be driven by linear and analytical thought. They are more methodical in their reasoning, thinking in words and focusing on facts and logic. The secret to creativity is not to be afraid to experiment. I can remember in art college loving the liberation of painting with sticks instead of brushes. We were also encouraged to draw the spaces in between objects, rather than the objects themselves. Magic happens when we allow ourselves to relax and let things flow, without worrying about the outcome.

Many of us would not consider ourselves to have a talent for creativity. But in truth, creativity is just utilising the imagination. You are being creative far more than you might realise. Every time you're changing or making something, you are creating, including the meals you prepare, the garden you tend to, and the house that you decorate. Some of the greatest artists have employed the simplest techniques to create their masterpieces, such as Piet Mondrian's flat planes of colour. If you have an urge to explore creating in any form - from working with clay, designing jewellery, or painting models, to taking up a life drawing or cake decorating class - make it happen. Your soul will thank you for it.

Archangel Gabriel, as the Messenger Angel, can also help with all forms of communication. Public speaking is the number one fear for people. Resiliency is what you muster up when you refuse to give up. No one can carry your dream better than you, and it can only come through you. You are enough. Your life is meant to leave an indelible impression on others. When you are prepared for others to witness your authenticity, you will be truly liberated.

Speaking is the doorway to having your needs met, and your desires manifested. It's also the doorway to how you can pour life and vitality into the most people possible. There are three types of people in this world – those that you come away from feeling uplifted by, the neutral types that don't affect you, and, finally, energy vampires that suck the life out of you. Be conscious of how you communicate with others. Consider how you want others to feel and think when you connect with them. Your voice can give power where someone may have felt weak, to lift others' hearts, to provide hope to the hopeless, and provide vision and clarity for a brighter future.

Communication is the distance between you and everything you desire, so make sure you have an impact and utilise your voice. Your voice can open up possibilities. Give yourself permission to breathe life into people and own the responsibility that comes with it.

Fear is a made-up story about something that is in the future. Fear is not the enemy, so don't allow it to stop you in your tracks. It's an emotion, and it is letting us know that we either need to get more information, or it is telling us to slow down. Ask the fear what it needs so that it can dissipate. Fear has come from a story that you have made up; make up a new story instead, one where you are smashing life and being wildly successful. When you permit yourself to fail, you allow yourself to fly. When you are so afraid of failing that you never take the leap, you won't ever fail, but neither will you fly.

When you're speaking to a group of people, you're really only talking to one person. Inspire the group, one person at a time. Get out of your ego that worries about how you look and sound, and place all your attention on serving your audience. Connect to them and think about what they need and what they are asking for. In the spirit of service, you will never fail. Take the fear with you; don't wait for it to leave you. Don't allow it to rob you of your happiness. It's normal to be afraid, but also remember that the body can't tell the difference between being afraid or excited. Tell yourself that this is something you have chosen to do, and remember the reasons why you want to do it.

When you are speaking, strengthening your message through movement engages the audience so that they feel what you are saying. Your message should come through you. You are more than an intellectual being. You have not come here to be a walking encyclopaedia. You do not have to remember everything word for word. Your passion needs to be shown - and felt - through movement and expression. Engage your body so that you offer all of yourself, and, in return, your audience will offer all of themselves. I learned from the beautiful Lisa Nichols to see our body as an orchestra where your performance is a symphony. Your voice is the song, and your body is the instrument. Allow them to find their own rhythm and perform as one. Explore your full range, and practise over expressing yourself, as well as experimenting with different voice styles, such as going from reading a children's story to presenting the news. By opening yourself up, you will find your true authentic style. Fully engage yourself, and you will fully engage your audience.

AFFIRMATIONS FOR ARCHANGEL GABRIEL

'Thank you, Archangel Gabriel, for releasing all worry and nervousness and giving me superior speaking skills.'

'Thank you, Archangel Gabriel, for divinely guiding me in my writing.'

'Thank you, Archangel Gabriel, for restoring peace and calmness when my children are tired and cranky.'

'Thank you, Archangel Gabriel, for helping me to be an extraordinary parent, and for watching over my children.'

This Scented Healing Mist is herbal, earthy and grounding, with a harmony of sage, dry lavender and rich vetiver. These provide rich herbal and earthy tones, connecting you with mother Earth.

Chapter 7:
Archangel Uriel

Insights and Intellectual Pursuits

Super Powers	Increase your confidence in your own intelligence and wisdom / Help you with important conversations / Spark new ideas and solutions / Assist with problem solving and brainstorming / Develop your psychic powers and intuitive skills
Name Translation	Light of God
Crystal	Amber, Hematite, Obsidian, Tiger's Eye, Rutilated Quartz
Colour	Red, purple or gold flecked with ruby
Helping People	Brings the light of the sun when you're feeling drained. Encourages us to shine our light and be our most authentic self.
Ray	6th Gold Ray representing peace

Archangel Uriel can bring in the flashes of inspiration and creativity that are needed to propel us on our journey of success. His name comes from the Hebrew for 'God's Light', 'Light of God' or 'the Fire of God', and he can help us get answers to questions. When you call on Archangel Uriel's help, notice your thoughts. You can trust what you get is the right answer. He is known as 'The Epiphany Angel' as he offers such great ideas and guidance. Uriel is associated with claircognisance, meaning clear knowing, and linked to the crystal amber.

Archangel Uriel comes in on the gold ruby red 6th ray. He has a red light but is also associated with the colour yellow. He is known as the Angel of wisdom, and gives sparks of inspiration and new insight. He brings the light of the sun to replenish your energy, especially when you feel drained. His message to us is to shine our light as he encourages us to be our most authentic self.

For help to increase your confidence in your intelligence and wisdom, and to help you with important conversations, ask Archangel Uriel. He can help spark new ideas and solutions, and assist with problem-solving and brainstorming. He helps with mental functioning, including focus and concentration. He can help you develop your psychic powers and intuitive skills, providing insight through visions, dreams and sudden perceptions.

Inspiration can only come to us when our mind is quiet. We live in a world that bombards us with information fighting for our attention. Many of us are usually glued to our phones, tablets, televisions or computers. Most of the time, we are not fully present as we work through our 'to-do' lists, planning for the next thing we have to achieve. Our monkey minds are rarely still.

The most beneficial thing we can do for ourselves is the regular practise of meditation. The mind is like a muscle that we have to train to serve us. Left to its own devices, it will run on default, continually looking for dangers and threats.

Many mistake meditation for the act of clearing the mind of all thought. While that may be the ultimate goal, meditation can also be the simple act of focusing on a physical sensation, such as watching the breath or repeating a mantra. Thoughts will interfere, and by noticing, we can return to the act of focus. Those that can apply this disciplined act of attention to their everyday lives can achieve anything that they desire. Most of us sleep 7-hours a day, which leaves us with 17 waking hours. Imagine now that you were to spend 14 of those hours practising playing the piano. How good would you be after six months? It pays to get clear about what you desire and dedicate your focus to achieving it.

Meditation doesn't just have to be sitting still and counting your breath. Try active meditations where you focus entirely on a task in hand, such as walking or washing the dishes. Be fully immersed in that action, engaging all the senses. You may also like to try chanting, or any form of focused intention.

Thoughts will still appear, and the trick is to let them float by without attachment. The moments of silence in between are where the sparks of inspiration will appear. This is when we can connect to our soul and receive guidance from above.

ALIGNING WITH THE FLOW

You are a being with no end to your capacity for expansion. We have the gift to be able to watch what we most think about turn into reality. For this reason, we must treat our thoughts as if they were spells of magic.

Let your last thought at night and first thing in the morning be for the appreciation of the small things that don't challenge you in any way, such as the feeling of the pillow under your head. I always begin each morning by giving thanks to the Angels for all their love and support, and asking that there be no limits to the amount of help they give me. I do this as soon as I am ready to open my eyes.

It's easier to start the day in appreciation if you've ended the previous day in appreciation; you then wake up in the same state. Similarly, it's easier to have a better day if you've started it in appreciation, as the Law of Attraction is amplifying your current state. Esther Hicks explains this as being in the vortex, essentially finding a state of joy and bliss. From there, everything flows.

Making and holding your relationship with the Universe at this level is the most beneficial thing you can do if you want to have a life full of abundance. The challenge is to not put your focus on the things you don't want. Personally speaking, as an empath, this can be a lot easier said than done. Our natural state, when we see someone in pain, is to sympathise with them. But in fact, we are of no benefit in doing so; the thoughts of what is, when the 'what is' isn't what they want, do not need amplifying further. This does not mean, of course, that we need to shut off our emotions; instead we hold the best version of people and situations. If we genuinely care and want to make a difference, the best action we can take is to hold the space for things to shift. Tell someone they are amazing, and they will become amazing! I believe this is how the Angels see us - as the best possible versions - and maintaining this focus brings us into alignment and closer to them.

As a healer, I hold the space for people to move into perfect health by seeing them as so. It's easy to get sucked into the reactive state of feeling sorry for yourself or others when things go wrong. It takes great strength to take a step back and ask, as the deliberate creator of your life, why you have brought what is not wanted into your existence, then make the conscious decision to realign.

Thoughts and feelings have a specific magnetic energy, which attracts energy of a similar nature. We can see this in action when we 'accidentally' bump into someone that we have just been thinking about, or 'happen' to pick up a book that contains the exact message we need to hear at that moment. These synchronistic moments are signs that we are in alignment with our true state of being.

Our thoughts need to be treated as magic because they are the first step to manifestation. When we create something, we always create it first in a thought-form. Our thoughts then act as a blueprint, creating an image of the form, which magnetises and guides the physical energy to flow into that form, and eventually manifest into the physical plane. 'Abracadabra!' – which literally translates as 'I create what I speak.'

What would you do if you knew you could not fail? How different would life be if you existed and experienced it from a state of love instead of fear? The reality is that, here on Earth, we are safe, guided and protected, in spite of appearances to the contrary. Everything we need is already within us as thought-form that rapidly materialises. The key when we're unsure is to ask for help and to not allow fear to immobilise us. We are given the act of free will, and guidance can only be given if we ask for it. If ever you are feeling stuck, afraid or unsure, hand the situation over to God, let the Angels guide you, and get out of your own way. A problem cannot be solved with the same mindset that created it. Worry and fear only bring you more of the same. Shift your focus to visualise what it would feel like to have what you need, and stop focusing on what is missing. In manifesting, be as clear as you can about what you require and desire. Be passionate about it happening. Visualise it and how you will feel once it is delivered. Send out your requests and then forget about it, but believe it will come true for you.

Know that your Angels are always with you. Their guidance usually comes through as whispers of intuition. An excellent way to feel their connection is to ask for signs to let us know that they are with us. These can come in all manner of experiences, and the most common is to find feathers. I have such a passion for finding feathers that even my children find them for me now, and I have a drawer full of them.

Another clear sign that our Angels are with us is to see repeated numbers. Today, for example, I looked at the clock at 11.11am – a sign from my Angels that I am in line with the Universe, and my thoughts are manifesting quickly into form. Doreen Virtue's bestselling book *Angel Numbers 101* gives excellent insight into the meaning of number sequences, as does *Angel Numbers* by Kyle Gray.

While out walking my dogs, I have asked the Angels for specific signs. Wanting it to be something unusual to make it more special, I asked for heart-shaped stones that I could fit in my hand. I now have a whole collection!

Music is another common form of communication from our Angels. Perhaps you've noticed the lyrics of a song for the first time and felt they were a message to you just when you needed to hear it? These synchronistic moments can happen through various channels, such as finding the perfect book, or noticing a car number plate with a key phrase. We receive countless messages every day, once we learn to pay attention. They serve as beautiful reminders that we are on track and fully supported.

The Angels are in constant communication with us through thoughts and feelings. Quite often, we need to get out of our own way to pick up on such guidance. Meditation helps slow down the mind, allowing the Angels to better communicate with us. We can tune into them in the space between thoughts.

MEDITATION AND BREATHING EXERCISE

Begin by taking a long, slow, deep breath in. Now, try some invigorating rhythmic breathing known as prana yam. Take two short inhales through your nostrils and two short exhales out of your nostrils as rhythmically as you can. Do this for a few minutes, preferably with your eyes closed. All prana yam is intended to nourish you, but if you start to feel dizzy, stop. Always listen to your body. Try this for a few rounds, it should feel quite invigorating.

You can slow your body and mind down to prepare for meditation by shortening the inhale and lingering the exhale. This calms the vagus nerve that connects to the fight or flight part of the brain. Start by breathing in for the count of four, and out for the count of six. Do this for a few rounds then extend it to breathing in for the count of six and out for the count of eight.

You can also try alternate nostril breathing, using your ring finger and your thumb. Hold closed the right nostril and breath out through the left nostril. Then breath in through the left nostril, float at the top of the inhale, and switch sides, so closing the left nostril and breathing out through the right nostril. Floating at the bottom of the exhale and breathing back in through the right nostril. You can picture the breath coming up from the bottom of the spine on the inhale, and out through the centre of the forehead on the exhale. Repeat this cycle for a couple of minutes. Then return to taking a long, slow, deep breath in, and gently let that that go. Slowly, follow the breath in and out.

Many people believe that they can't do meditation because they think that they can't block out their thoughts. But meditation is simply the act of focus and expanded awareness. After a few rounds of breathing exercises, bring your attention to your senses. Close your eyes and start by becoming aware of everything that you can hear. Then notice what you can taste. What can you smell? Even with your eyes closed, what can you see? Bring your attention to everything that you can feel; fine tune sensations right to the tips of the hairs on your body. Now, bring all those senses together in symphony.

My personal favourite is to repeat a mantra. This can be as simple as just a word, such as 'one', or any affirmation you choose. Place your awareness outside of yourself as you settle into the flow. Your mind will jump in with thoughts, but rather than getting swept along with them, bring your awareness back to the mantra.

Afterwards, go on to raise your vibration even further by thinking about something that you can feel truly grateful for, and give thanks for that. Picture someone that you love and send out love to them. Then, share that love with the rest of the world. Whatever you send out will be brought back to you.

By surrendering to a daily meditation where we can quieten ourselves, we can merge into oneness. Only in these quiet moments can we truly hear the whispers of the Angels.

AFFIRMATIONS FOR ARCHANGEL URIEL

'Thank you, Archangel Uriel, for giving me the insights and epiphanies just as I need them.'

'Thank you, Archangel Uriel, for giving me all the information I need to be on my path of purpose.'

'Thank you, Archangel Uriel, for giving me clarity of thought and laser focus.'

'Thank you, Archangel Uriel, for filling me with infinite wisdom and understanding.'

This Scented Healing Mist is a blend of sparkling bright grapefruit with bright, fresh spice of ginger, grounded in white woods and peppermint to give transparency and clarity.

CHAPTER 8:
ARCHANGEL ZADKIEL

Violet Flame, Memory and Emotional Healing

Super Powers	Remembering Facts and Figures / Emotional Healing / Remember your Divine Spiritual Origin / Transform Negative Thoughts and Feelings / Dissolve Karma
Name Translation	The Righteousness of God
Crystal	Blue Lace Agate, Amethyst, Blue Chalcedony, Lapis Lazuli
Colour	Sky blue, indigo blue, violet
Helping People	Assists in transformation with alternative medical fields, including Reiki masters, masseurs, aromatherapists, psychiatrists. Also students with exams to take and anyone struggling with memory. Anyone struggling with emotions. Help with remembering what's important and to be able to focus on what matters most. Developing diplomacy and tolerance for all with the power of mercy

and transformation.

Ray   7th Violet Ray for freedom

Archangel Zadkiel, meaning 'The Righteousness of God', is known as one of the angels of justice and mercy. He comes in on the 7th violet ray carrying the violet flame, the ray of forgiveness and purification. The violet flame is a spiritual energy that we can imagine around us to get rid of all negativity, heal the heart, and bring out our own higher Angelic qualities, making our inner light shine brighter. This energetic violet flame can be called upon to burn away anything that is holding us back in fear. It has a powerful ability to transmute anything held in fear, moving it back into love. If ever you feel challenged or held back, call upon Archangel Zadkiel to help you move through with ease and grace. Although he is an Angel that is surrounded by violet fire, he is an incredibly gentle Angel that comes in peace. He is wonderful for help in emotional healing. Archangel Zadkiel can also help our memory, so is great to call upon if you have a test where you need to know facts or dates, for example.

Vibrant Zadkiel can uplift us to have the courage to make changes in our life. Even change for the better can be scary, but it helps to stay focused on his powerful energy that brings opportunities for freedom and joy. Zadkiel can help us address all negativity with the gift of transformation. Focusing on his violet light will help us to let go of harsh self-judgement and cleanses us from limiting thoughts. This opens us up to find joy and positivity in every situation.

With seemingly so much pain and suffering in the world, it can often be overwhelming for empaths to cope. We feel like we should be aware of all the tragedy going on around us, but in doing so, we're lowering our own vibration which has a ripple effect. The news is designed to report only negative stories to keep us locked in a state of fear. It acts like a drug, keeping us hooked as the amygdala gland in our brain fires off emotional responses to keep us engaged. Good will stories rarely, if ever, make the news. There are no cameras to capture the fact that there have been no aeroplane crashes that day, or no shootings in a school. The truth is, the world is getting safer and, on the whole, we are surrounded by wonderful people. By not watching the news, we can be of greater help to the world as we concentrate on keeping our inner strength and vibration high, creating a positive impact that radiates. The maharishi effect was observed when just 1% of the population practised meditation, which lowered the crime rate by an average of 16%. By all means, don't ignore the pain and suffering if you're in an active position to do something about it. But allowing yourself to be a helpless bystander as you passively absorb negativity does nothing to help anyone.

With that being said, it's important not to suppress our emotions; this adds to the layers that keep us separated from our true essence of pure love as powerful energetic beings. Emotional guidance lets you know that you are not yet up to speed with that which you have become. Your emotions let you know where your vibration is at so that you can recalibrate and alter your course. Our emotions act as a compass, letting us know exactly where we are. Everything that is happening in your life experience is coming in response to your vibrational level.

EMOTIONAL INTELLIGENCE

Emotional intelligence is incredibly important. Life is filled with disappointments and failures. At various stages, life is going to challenge us, whether it's parenting a difficult teen, starting our own business, or coping with grief, for example. When confronted with such issues, having the emotional resilience to be able to keep trying and keep going is imperative.

The trick is not to be fearful of failure and fall into the trap of being tentative about life. Those who have been brought up in a sheltered environment, or only ever given praise, risk putting pressure upon themselves to achieve to get the recognition and acceptance they crave. They lose sight of all enjoyment and eventually hit burn out.

Our beliefs are magnetic, and they draw into our lives that what we believe about ourselves. It's important to realise that beliefs are not facts, even though we treat them as such. If a belief is not serving you, do stop to question what that belief means to you or means about you. Ask yourself, what would you rather believe? Consider the possibilities in life if you chose to uphold a new belief instead.

Think about the bigger picture of your actions and functions. Even the challenges you face are a gift, and if it doesn't feel like it, you haven't got to the end. `There are no negative emotions. Fear, frustration, hate, anger, and guilt all serve a purpose if you look upon them as messages to act quickly to change the situation. Get curious as to what your emotion has to offer you. What is the real message it is giving you? Emotions are our sixth sense. We should not try to resist them because what we resist persists. Be open and honest about your emotions and learn to work with them.

Emotions can be seen as vibrational feedback that helps us navigate between where we are now and where we want to go. Embrace all emotions, good and bad, as they are the barometer for where you are at. Acceptance is the first step to make progress in life. We must risk our vulnerability to express what we truly feel. Emotions mustn't be just dismissed or brushed over. They need to be validated and seen as important. If someone is experiencing pain, do not try and distract them or avoid the issue. Listen empathetically in an attempt to understand the way they feel. Allow them to feel and experience their emotion fully before moving forward towards any improvement in the way that they feel. Support them without trying to fix them.

After their feelings have been fully acknowledged and fully felt, then you can help the other person strategise ways to manage the reactions they may be having to their emotion. Below are a few suggestions on how to do this.

Fear is an indication that you need to prepare for something. Rewire your brain to move away from pain and move towards pleasure by focusing on what it is that you do want, rather than what you don't.

If you feel hurt, this indicates that your expectations have not been met. Again, shift your focus onto what you do want instead. Change your communication and communicate your needs better, or meet someone else's needs better.

Anger lets you know that you have a significant rule that's been violated. Anger can be a useful state to get you moving up and out of the feeling of helplessness.

Frustration says that what you're doing isn't working. You can still succeed, but you need to change or be more flexible.

Disappointment shows that something didn't go as expected. Instead, focus on what you want now.

Guilt indicates that you've violated one of your own standards. This is a sure-fire way to wake you up so that you don't ever do it again.

Feeling overwhelmed, helpless or depressed? This is a feeling of lack of freedom, of being out of control. On the other end of the scale is empowerment. That's where you find joy, appreciation and passion. Sit down and re-prioritise. Write a list of what you could do right now to start feeling better. Take back control by taking action. Do one thing on that list well and feel a sense of achievement.

If you are feeling alone, then this is a message that you need to connect with people.

If you're feeling inadequate, this is a message that you need to change your standards because you're being unfair to yourself. Commit to mastering this area. You're not going to be perfect first time.

***

Most of us deal with emotions by either avoiding them altogether, which becomes even more painful and creates a sense of loss. Some indulge in them, hanging onto them and pushing them down. Some compete to see who feels the worst, falling into comparative suffering as they argue over who 'has it worse'. Others try and share their pain, believing they can get rid of their emotions by offloading onto others. These are not intelligent ways to use our emotions. Instead, we have to change what they mean to us so that we can transform that feeling. Venting, demanding and expressing pain does not help in the long term.

Aim to create a healthy emotional environment. Don't be afraid to express your love. We live in a touch starved world as part of the illusion of separation. I offer Indian Head Massage treatments as I firmly believe in the power of touch. It is profoundly relaxing on mental and emotional levels as well as physical levels. There are many ways to show love. You may like to give gifts or help out. Quality time, giving your undivided attention, is a fabulous thing to do. All relationships can be nourished through the giving of attention, appreciation and affection.

Listen to and respect your own feelings. Get to know what you like and what you don't like. Your feelings are speaking your truth, and it's important to honour your emotions.

We all have something that we want that causes us pain until we get it. This could be a relationship, a better house or a job, for example. We all have a sense of not being fulfilled, and this is what drives us. But you can't solve an internal problem with external action. We first have to learn how to feel happy and complete, regardless. Then we are free to choose what we want to have in our lives. Realise that your life, with all the problems you think you have, is already perfect. In difficult times, ask yourself – are you being the person that you want to be? Does your current behaviour reflect this vision of yourself? If not, you know what to do to turn things around.

Living in a 'me' centred universe, you'll live a mediocre, frustrated existence with flashes of joy. Find something to benefit a larger group, and you will live a remarkable life.

To be genuinely successful, live a life based on love, not fear, including a love for yourself. Shine your light, be yourself and follow what lights you up. Let your emotions be your guidance system to align you with what you desire.

All manifestations begin with the end result. It's essential to focus on that and not the details. The 'how' is best left to the Universe to work out. If the groundwork to feeling worthy and deserving of your desires has been done, success is inevitable, provided action is taken.

You'll feel that you'll have truly conquered life if you appreciate the actions you take along the way, rather than focusing on lack in the present moment, or distress that you've not yet reached your goals. Many people attain their goal to find that they don't feel the sense of fulfilment that they imagined. Perhaps they were searching for external validation. Value based on productivity will always be illusive. The famous actor, Jim Carey, is quoted as saying that he wishes that 'everyone could become rich and famous so that they could realise that it's not the answer to happiness.' Realise that worth is inherent as you are an extension of Source energy. Your worth doesn't have to be justified. You can choose to showcase your light, or hide it. The angels want to remind you that you are enough at this very moment and in every moment.

Focus on yourself and others with an attitude of what you appreciate instead of what you condemn; in this way, you will know worth and joy. The Law of Attraction states that, what you focus on and find vibrational alignment with, will manifest in your experience. This is why it's imperative to hold thoughts of what you want, rather than what you don't. Everything in your life is giving you feedback as to where your vibration is. You get what you think about, whether you want it or not. The world is your mirror. Attention to the subject is what activates the Law of Attraction. Becoming continuously aware of our thought processes and catching ourselves when we are not in alignment with our authentic essence is quite a skill to master. The practise of mindfulness sharpens this ability, as we learn to be fully present in the moment, rather than being driven by the subconscious. Replace, 'Why is this happening to me?' with 'What is this trying to teach me?', then watch everything shift. Challenge yourself to go a whole day without complaining and see what a difference it makes, not only to yourself, but to those around you.

TIPS FOR MEMORY

Archangel Zadkiel is wonderful for help with our memory. As mentioned previously, the brain is nearly 70% fat, and it needs the healthy fats of omega oils to keep it healthy and stop it from shrinking. I take flaxseed oil for omega 3, 6 and 9. Early and regular consumption can ward off Alzheimer's and dementia in later life.

Memory recall can be improved by exercises like mnemonics. Songs, rhymes, acronyms, images or phrases can be used to remember chunks of information. This technique is particularly useful when the order of things is important.

We're particularly good at recognising pictures that we've seen before. Think about how many signs, symbols and logos that you can identify in a split second. When you meet someone new, spend a few seconds associating an image with their name.

Strong memories can also be created by combining multiple senses. Some of our most powerful recollections are encoded through smell, taste and touch sensations, as much as through sight and sound. Use all of your senses.

Imagine that you're learning about a new concept at work. Visualise it as a physical model and create as many different sensory routes as you can to lead you back to the original information.

Emotion is incredibly useful in memory recall. Be as creative as possible with associating important ideas in playful and mischievous ways to make things impossible to forget.

As mentioned, patterns and rhymes are another wonderful tool for memory. I manage to remember my phone number by breaking it down into small chunks and making a little song out of it. Another memory tip is to imagine your home, and assign different parts of what you're wanting to remember to different rooms. Then, picture yourself walking from room to room to remember what you need to.

Acronyms are also useful. One of the most well-known is used for remembering the colours of the rainbow - Richard Of York Gave Battle In Vein - relating to red, orange, yellow, green, blue, indigo and violet. Being able to pick up skills quickly is vital in today's environment. Whether you're a student, professional, parent or retiree, all of us need to learn new things every day.

Have you ever wondered why you can read a page and then find you have forgotten what you have read about? The key to overcoming this is to ask yourself questions. Make the information relatable to you. Ask yourself how you can use that information? Make the information relevant. Ask yourself why you need to know that information? Then put it into context. When will you use that information? When you're trying to absorb information, do so from the perspective that you're going to go on and teach about it. It gives you a different standpoint to pay attention better.

It can be a gut-wrenching moment when you need to introduce someone but you've completely forgotten their name. Or perhaps you're in a meeting and it's your turn to speak, but the vital information has escaped you. Linking images, senses, emotions and patterns to what you want to remember is the key to success. If you want to have things stored in your long-term memory, practise over and over with repetition and link emotion to the information. Even just rehearsing things in your mind has the same effect. Try these techniques out while you're reading this book. How can you apply what you've learned here to your life?

THE BENEFITS OF SELF LOVE

Archangel Zadkiel is the Angel of mercy and transformation. If we want to change the world, we must first change our self. Realise that loving yourself is a short cut to enlightenment. Every single brand of spiritual practise out there is geared towards loving yourself. The best state you can align with is that of pure positive focus. We are here to become more of who we truly are. This requires awareness. All the great teachers of the world will tell you that everything you want can be found within yourself. When we try to satisfy our emotional needs externally, we will always be left wanting.

Recognise that you are a divine spirit, and you are worthy of love. The very fibre of your being is pure unconditional love; it cannot be any other way. The very fact you exist means you are worthy. Existence doesn't make mistakes. I saw a lovely post on social media. It was a note from someone who had just connected with her body to ask it what it needed. She thought the response might be to drink more water, exercise more, or eat organic food. Instead, her body asked her to look at herself in the mirror and said, 'Can you love me like this?' This poignant question requires total self-acceptance. None of us are perfect, and wouldn't life be boring if we were! Appreciate what your body does for you; nurture it and connect with it in ways that make it feel good.

I love this quote by Teal Swan:-

'I want you to imagine that each person is in a room with a canvas in the middle of that room. Most people begin to paint unconsciously because it seems like the only thing to do. Some then begin to paint whatever gets them commission, but they do so with dread because it isn't what they really want to paint. Others, who call themselves spiritual, go through the motions of painting, but dream endlessly about what is outside of that room. It is the rare person who begins to consciously paint on that canvas and paint what they truly desire to paint. It is rare because most people have forgotten they are painters and the canvas is called life.'

When someone figures out how to be themselves, it is the most liberating, life-affirming experience possible. Growing up is a painful process as we learn to become comfortable in our own skin. Fear of judgment and feelings of not fitting in can cause us to abandon our self and even question our own self-worth. But deep down we all have our own sense of strength and power. Every single one of us comes to this world with our own uniqueness, and yet there is always more that unites us than divides us. Being willing to be seen for our authentic self is our one true strength that will set us free.

You're amazing at being yourself when you're a child. You are only aware of yourself and you don't know how to describe your differentness. If you ask a class of four-year-olds who the strongest boy is, all the hands will go up. Each one will like to think that they are strong. If you do the same in a class of 7-year-olds, they'll point to someone and say, 'He's the strongest', or 'he's the cleverest', and so on. Societal archetypes emerge around the age of seven, as this is when the birth of social consciousness happens, when we suddenly become more aware of what is on the outside of us. That's why the saying goes, 'Give me a boy until the age of seven and I'll show you the man.' From then on, as you become more aware of the world around you, you become more self-conscious and less good at being yourself.

The other time you're amazing at being yourself is when you're old and wrinkly because by then you can't be bothered. You realise there are more summers behind you than there are in front of you, and everything intensifies. You become more honest. You become less compromising. We might call them being eccentric, but in fact, what they are doing is being more authentic.

It's that bit in the middle that is the most difficult. This is where we have to socialise, accommodate and adapt. Your entire life has been about building a stable relationship with your ego. If we have a fragile ego, we may develop a complex. Having an inferiority complex is suffering from delusions of insignificance. Having a superiority complex is having delusions of grandeur. Your challenge is to take the ego from its dominant position and pull it back so it's of service to yourself. Finding the equilibrium is the key to remaining impervious to all the good and bad that happens to you and keeping a sense of humility. Humility is not thinking less of yourself; it's thinking about yourself less.

Learn to be okay with your past. Realise that everything you have been through has led you to your awakening of who you are on a deeper level. Try and redirect your focus to what is wanted rather than play a victim role. We are who we choose to be in this moment now. The Universe is waiting for you to direct it.

You're not just somebody's boss or somebody's mum, or somebody's anything for that matter. Often, we can suffer from approval addiction. The need to be liked, recognised, or for someone to tell you it's okay. People will always have a perception of you, and this will vary. We can't escape that. But we can be perception free. There is a part of us that is changing all the time. When people say they have 20 years' experience, often they are saying that they've done the same thing over and over again for twenty years. Your job is to be better and better at being who you already are. Most of us, however, would rather sleepwalk until something happens to wake us up. But when we wait for something catastrophic to rock us back into awakening, we're at our most vulnerable and weakest state. Why not ask yourself these questions when you are strong? If you could be the man / woman of your dreams, who would you be?

CREATE AN INSPIRING VISION FOR YOUR LIFE

See in great detail what you want in your future by asking yourself the following questions.

1. What really excites you?

2. What are you passionate about?

3. What contribution do you want to make to the world?

4. What do you want to be remembered for?

5. What unique talents do you have to offer the world?

Now project yourself twenty-five years into the future.

6. What accomplishments do you want to look back on with pride?

7. What do you need to have done for you to feel that you have lived a full life where you have lived to your full potential?

8. How will you have maximised all your talents?

Write the answers out to these questions somewhere you can refer back to them. Create a vision board that you can see every day to be a constant reminder to yourself of what matters most to you.

Even when you are born without many of the attributes and advantages that your peers have, by tapping into your inner voice and harnessing your uniqueness, you can achieve great things. You are a powerful being with an important life mission to fulfil. Step into your own personal power, and don't be afraid to express yourself. By delving into what makes you *you*, not only will the substance of your life get richer, but you will never feel superfluous again.

Take the time now to connect with yourself. The heart is your connection to your higher self. When you stop and listen to your heart, you align with your true desires for expansion.

AFFIRMATIONS FOR ARCHANGEL ZADKIEL

'Thank you, Archangel Zadkiel, for helping me recall all the information that I need to know about this topic.'

'Thank you, Archangel Zadkiel, for healing my mind and shifting me to a more peaceful and loving state.'

'Thank you, Archangel Zadkiel, for inspiring forgiveness and compassion.'

'Thank you, Archangel Zadkiel, for helping me to practise unconditional love and kindness.'

This Scented Healing Mist has notes of grapefruit and sweet violet, paired with a subtle herbal lavender. A harmony of bright fresh spices of cardamom and ginger add an uplifting, vibrant aura. The balance of sweet floral and soft spice give a healing tonality. Many remark that this scent is reminiscent of Palma Violets

CHAPTER 9:
ARCHANGEL AZRAEL

Angel of Comfort and Grief, Endings and Transitions, Mediumship

Super Powers	Heals grief / Healing of the heart / Mediumship
Name Translation	He who is Helped by God. Whom God Helps
Crystal	Yellow Calcite, Amethyst, Purple Fluorite
Colour	Light shade of vanilla, coral
Helping People	Councillors, the clergy, healers, psychic mediums. Helping people and animals to cross over into spirit. Assistance in delivering a Eulogy.
Attributes	Quiet, composed and patient with a self-loving energy

If you're burdened with sorrow, have suffered loss or need comfort, call upon Azrael. He is the most graceful and elegant of all the Archangels, and his name means 'He is Helped by God' or 'Whom

God helps'. Azrael helps those who are helpers, particularly those that support the grieving or dying. If you are comforting an animal or person through the last days of their life, ask for Archangel Azrael's assistance. He can also help you remain compassionate and patient with any aspect of counselling.

CONNECTING WITH THE SPIRIT WORLD

Archangel Azrael assists our soul in transitioning between worlds. For this reason, he is also a wonderful guide for those practising mediumship. As half of my family have passed over, the art of mediumship is something that deeply fascinates me. If you are grieving for a loved one, I highly recommend the Talking to Heaven cards by James Van Praagh, and also the book The Top Ten Things Dead People Want to Tell You by Mike Dooley. These have brought me incredible comfort and insight into what it must be like on the other side. Our loved ones are only ever a thought away, and I continue to talk to my loved ones telepathically with the knowledge that they can hear me.

I've been blessed with some amazing moments of connection from my departed family. My brother had been very ill all his adult life through alcohol and substance abuse. Crippled by acute anxiety, he no longer knew how to be in life. Not long after his premature death, I remember standing at the sink in the utility room when, all of a sudden, I could smell stale alcohol. I thought, 'Edward, is that you?' Then, in the next moment, I was washed over with the most incredible feeling of peace and pure bliss. I know that this was him reassuring me that he was finally in a good place, and not to worry about him anymore.

Some months later, we were having a special family breakfast of pancakes and my two children were busy setting the table. We have inherited a beautiful round oak table with five chairs. The children had set a place for every chair, even though there were only four of us. When we noticed I remarked, 'It's ok, Uncle Edward can have that place.' A few weeks later, my mum and I went to visit a gifted medium. Totally unprompted, she told me that Edward had been really pleased that we had set a place for him at the table. I was blown away! It is such an amazing comfort to know that he is around us.

People say that you have to be born with a gift to be a medium. I believe that it's possible to train yourself to become open to spirit. I have attended many circles to try and develop this practice. I have been taught that it is important to first open up your energy by raising your vibration. The trick is to learn to stand in your own power and hold that energy, then blend with the Spirit energy around you. You can raise your vibration through music and meditation. You can open yourself up by visualising yourself surrounded by white light. You are setting the intention to communicate clearly with spirit. I know when spirit is with me as the hairs on my head stand up. Sometimes, you can feel sensations on the body such as a feeling of cobwebs on the skin, or heavy muscles. The atmosphere in the room changes. Quite often, people take on the physical symptoms of those that have passed over, but once they have given a message from them, this disappears. The art is in giving whatever comes to you without question. It's working purely from the right side of the brain where intuition lives. There is no rationalising or analysing here. You will be amazed at what seemingly illogical facts can make the world of difference to someone who has been given that message.

The difference between a great medium and the average medium is how well they translate information through their Clairs.

Clairvoyance is the art of seeing. This all happens within the mind, so it's receiving mental images that pop into the mind. This is a skill that can be practised with the art of visualisation. Try thinking about something, closing your eyes, and holding that vision. Many people say they can't do this, but if I asked to you picture your front door, that image will come to you. This is exactly how Spirit will communicate – by showing you images in your mind.

Clairsentience is the ability to feel anything that Spirit wishes to make you feel. You may become aware of personalities, emotions or illnesses. All we are doing here is monitoring for changes within ourselves. Once we have blended with Spirit we may, for example, become aware that we can't breathe, which indicates that the Spirit had a breathing condition.

Clairaudience is the ability to hear Spirit. This happens within the mind, so you don't hear Spirit in the same way you hear the living when they speak to you. It happens through thought. So, the Spirit's voice will sound like your own inner voice, and all you have to do is learn to tell the difference between your thoughts and those coming from Spirit.

It is possible to see Spirit with the physical eyes and hear with the physical ears, but 99.9% of time it will happen in the way just outlined. At the start of your journey, you may begin with one or two

Of the clairs. You will find that others will be introduced to you as you progress. The trick to becoming a good medium is learning to get the most out of the clairs.

Spirit can only communicate as well as the person who is able to translate the message. If you only have clairvoyance, you can only give what you see, but understand that there are other ways for Spirit to get their message across. They may show you an image of one of your friends to get a name across to you. Or they may show you your own mum so that you know you are connecting with a mother.

The secret is to stand in your own power and give up control and expectation, so that you're not looking for information and are simply allowing yourself to be a blank canvas. Let Spirit take full control of the message that you start to get through; don't get stuck in logically trying to understand it, just say it as it comes through. In this way, you'll find messages become highly evidential and entertaining, as well as powerful and healing.

Learn to translate thoughts and feelings. Think about how you would get a message across in the easiest way possible. If it's someone's birthday, you may picture a balloon or a cake, for example. Practise this translation while you're having regular conversations with people. If you're having an interesting conversation with someone, stop and consider how Spirit would translate that through the clairs. Spirit then know to use this translation when they wish to communicate something similar.

People receive information in a variety of ways. You may just know, you may hear, or you may see. When I am trying to connect, I place all my awareness outside of my body. I mentally connect with the energy around me. You may like to visualise a screen above your head and see what appears on that. At the end, give thanks and imagine that white light returning to Source. It is important to disconnect and not take that energy with you. Have fun playing with this. Free yourself up to be able to give a message by creating abstract imagery, such as encaustic wax art, or select different coloured ribbons and use these as prompts for messages. The more you can relax and let things flow, the more successful you will be.

COPING WITH CHANGE

As Archangel Azrael is the Angel of transition, he can help us leave behind what is holding us back so that we can step into a new beginning. We are creatures of habit and we can often find change unsettling, even if it is for the best. Archangel Azrael can help us cope with these difficult emotions, helping us move through transitions with ease and grace. He is one of the most graceful, loving and sweet Angels there is. You may be experiencing change through moving jobs, moving home, or dealing with a changing relationship, or perhaps you know someone ready to move on from this life. Archangel Azrael will be there at the perfect time to assist their soul in making the transition to the non-physical. Archangel Azrael will also comfort and support the grieving family, as well as anyone who is going through times of change.

My most challenging time in my life was coping with change after I was made redundant from my position of textile designer. I had only been back at work a month, following nine month's maternity leave, when I was informed that my position was no longer required. This came as a huge shock to me because, as far as I was concerned, I was busier than ever.

After fourteen years in the industry, I had grown accustomed to having a good regular income. Money had been very tight on maternity leave, and the redundancy settlement was not set to last more than a couple of months. My deepest desire to be able to send my child to a private school for the best education seemed to have disappeared in an instant. Now, I wasn't even sure if I was going to be able to afford the nappies he needed, or the clothes.

It wasn't just the financial insecurity that broke me, but also my loss of identity. Rightly or wrongly, a big part of who I was was linked to what I did for a living. After all, the first question anyone asks when they get to know you is, 'And what do you do?' I knew, as much as I wanted to be a mother, I didn't want that to be my soul purpose. The isolation I felt being a stay-at-home mum was all-consuming. Despite every measure I took to reprogramme my mind with hypnosis, the powerlessness I felt led to a deep depression.

One day, I was driving along a stretch of road that narrowed on the other side. The car coming the other way swerved out and hit my wing mirror, smashing the glass. That one little trigger was the breaking point. As I wondered how I was going to be able to pay for that on top of everything else, I burst into tears. Hours later, the tears couldn't stop. The flood gates had opened, and I realised that I had to seek medical help.

The medication helped me to lose weight, which made me feel

better about myself. Then, I began to realise that the side effects were starting to outweigh the benefits as they suppressed my enjoyment of life. Sometimes though we all need a little bit of help, just to get us through the worst of things, and we have to reach out and ask for it.

Things, of course, did improve. I came off the medication, and went on to have a second child, both of whom I'm blessed to say now attend a private school. I created my own business, enabling me to work my own hours around my children, taking care of my animals and enjoying time in the fresh air, as opposed to being stuck in front of a computer screen. I've learned to follow my passion, and I'm doing what gives me the most satisfaction in life, giving full expression to my dreams. I consider myself to be incredibly blessed. Change is never easy, even when it's the best for us. It helps us to realise that, if things don't work out as you hoped, it's only because the Universe has a better plan for you.

I remember a lovely lady coming to my stand at one of the mind, body, spirit events that I do, feeling very worried because Archangel Azrael had appeared to her. She knew he is associated as the Angel of Death. After reassuring her about all the ways Archangel Azrael can help, it transpired that she herself was a psychic medium! She was extremely relieved to discover that this beautiful, gentle Angel helps mediums connect to the other side. It is he who helps bring love and light to those of us on Earth. He has been associated with the colour coral - a colour linked to higher love - and also a yellow-cream colour. Holding or wearing the yellow calcite crystal may lend added comfort through Azrael's energy.

As humans, we tend not to cope too easily with change. Our brains are hardwired to look for familiarity. Change is, however, an inevitable constant in life, and our happiness depends upon our ability to adapt. Knowing that there are no guarantees, and nothing lasts forever, should make us appreciate every moment that we have.

When things don't work out as you had hoped, it's important to look beyond the immediate disappointment. Be mindful that you are being redirected towards something better than you could have anticipated. Affirm to yourself, 'Things are always working out for me,' and trust that the Universe really does have your best interests at heart. As painful as things may seem at the moment, all pain is temporary and things will improve. Trust that you are always being guided towards incredible opportunities for your soul's expansion and ultimate happiness.

Holding on to what was, or romanticising the past, blocks us from creating an even brighter future. Our memory can trick us into only remembering the good. The now is the only moment we have, so start caring about how you feel in this moment, and work out what makes you happy now.

In coping with change, it's hugely important to practise self-love and release resistance to alignment with your higher self. Caring for how you feel is undoubtedly an aspect of self-love. This includes doing things that make you feel happy and fulfilled. Having a healthy set of boundaries is also important. Actively take care of your body and nourish your mind and spirit. Be completely authentic in all that you do. Take the time to connect with yourself and listen to what you need, as getting those needs met is essential for your wellbeing.

HEALING THE HEART MEDITATION

'There can never be a spiritual authority outside of me that is greater than this voice I hear within, this is the voice of my own uncaged heart.'- *'Mary Magdalene Revealed', Meggan Watterson.*

With your eyes closed, place one hand on top of the other, straight over your heart. Your heart is located right under your sternum in the centre of your chest.

Breathe in and become aware of the energy of your heart. Your heart has its own energetic signature, along with every other organ in your body. You can learn to recognise this, just as you would a loved one, by how they make you feel. So, right now, recognise that unique energy of your heart.

Start to contemplate your heart as its own individual being. Connect with it now and feel the special energy that it has. Now imagine that it is a living, breathing being that has its own personality. This is a being that you can always relay on, one that you know always has your best interests in mind, like your North Star, always guiding you to what is true.

Now ask yourself, what does your heart want?

What does your heart dislike?

How does your heart feel? Does your heart feel appreciated and loved, or does it feel ignored and undervalued?

Just take some time now to be with your heart, exactly as it is, right here and now, without you needing it to be different.

You intuitively know how to communicate with your heart. There is no right or wrong way. It is part of you, constantly working hard to ensure your survival. Now take a few moments to get to know your heart a bit better.

Begin by asking four very important questions:-

What makes you unhappy?

What do you need me to do differently?

If you could have one wish, what would it be?

What do you have to tell me?

You will receive the answers on an intuitive level. Either you will hear the answers, or you will see them in your mind's eye, or you will know the answers as they will pop up in your consciousness.

Take a few minutes to reflect on the concerns your heart has expressed to you. Acknowledge in your mind's eye that you value its perspective and its wants and needs. Give your heart the reassurance it needs that the wishes it has expressed will be fulfilled. Keep in mind this might not be something that can be accomplished in one go. It might, for example, be a lifestyle change that your heart wants you to make.

Once you feel that you have reached a place of understanding with your heart, take some time to express gratitude for your heart, and for its particular purpose of working so hard to keep you alive. Visualise now that gratitude and love are flowing into your heart. Imagine that energy being soaked up by the heart and then pumped through the rest of the body. Imagine that love diffusing through all of the capillaries, the blood vessels, the arteries and veins, into every other organ; the heart is carrying the love there, throughout the totality of your being. Imagine that love soaking into each organ and every tiny little cell.

Just before you are ready to come back into the room, if you feel ready, make a promise to your heart that you will always be available to talk. Promise that you will fulfil its wishes, and that you agree with its perspective because you acknowledge the fact that it represents the truth of your being.

Now, take four deep breaths, inhaling the oxygen completely into your lungs, and allowing the oxygen to exit your lungs completely. After you've done this four times, you can wiggle your toes and your fingers, and come back into the room by opening your eyes.

Affirmations

'Thank you, Archangel Azrael, for helping me heal my heart, giving me the strength and courage to move on in my life.'

'Thank you, Archangel Azrael, for encouraging me to do something new or at least different every single day.'

'Thank you, Archangel Azrael, for helping me remain compassionate and patient with any aspect of counselling.'

'Thank you, Archangel Azrael, for helping me release all resistance to change so that I can fully embrace the life ahead of me.'

Chapter 10:
Archangel Orion

Wish upon a star/Manifestation

Super Powers A Galactic Angel with cosmic and love filled guidance from celestial realms / Gives us a better perspective / Connects us to our true desires / Manifest a life we love

Name Translation 'Rising in the Sky' - he is named from the three stars in the constellation Orion's Belt

Crystal Dark Blue Sandstone, Peacock Ore, Blue Goldstone, Lapis Lazuli

Colour Midnight blue with sparkles

Helping People Helps us see the big picture and ask big questions like, 'What do you really want to do while you're here on this planet? What do you want in relationships and in your family life?'

Attributes Expansive, connecting us to the vastness of the Universe.

Archangel Orion, named after the three stars in the constellation Orion's Belt, means 'Rising in the Sky'. He carries the energy of the stars and the Stellar Gateway that connects us to the power of the Universe.

When you think of Archangel Orion, think about wishing upon a star. We all believe that, if we make a wish upon a shooting star, it will come true. Well, this is the magical energy that Orion holds. He broadcasts healing light and frequency towards Earth through the centre of the three stars.

As the galactic Angel of the stars, Orion can help us make a wish and manifest what we need in this lifetime to be closer to our life purpose. He can help us connect with this potential, giving us a feeling of vastness and connectedness as we connect to something greater. When you're thinking about what you want to create and bring into reality, connect to Archangel Orion. The colour associated with him is a deep blue, like the night sky. So, crystals such as blue goldstone or lapis lazuli are ideal for helping to connect with him. His energy is expansive and feels like a big breath of fresh air.

Orion is one of the newer Archangels, and he helps us to connect to all that is, reminding us that we are one with everyone and everything in the entire Universe. By looking up to the sky, we can be reminded of the vastness of this Universe. Archangel Orion can help us connect to this unlimited potential, and help fulfil our wildest dreams in the most miraculous ways. He supports us on our ascension journey and to manifest a life that we love.

Archangel Orion encourages us to slow down, enjoy the moment, and define the things we want to create, with an understanding of why we want to create them. He enables us to have a greater sense of perspective, able to see the bigger picture and see what really needs to be focused on.

To invoke his energy, visualise yourself surrounded by stars; know that you are connected to the whole Universe.

Remember, miracles occur naturally. You are a magician, and you have the power to create the life you deserve. Whatever you put your focus upon is what will appear in your life.

YOU ARE STARDUST

When I visited the National Space Centre in Leicester, I watched the show at the planetarium. It explained how we are all made up of stardust. The atoms in our bodies come from the asteroids and comets of exploded stars that hit the Earth. It's incredible to consider when looking up at the night sky that we are connected to the fundamental fabric of the universe. We are the essence of the heavens above, and will always be a part of the materials from which the heavens are made.

This knowledge of connectedness can be extended even further to that of the collective consciousness. The greatest illusion is that of separation. There is a wonderful quote by Albert Einstein that I'd like to share with you.

'A human being is part of the whole, called by us the 'Universe', a part limited in time and space. He experiences himself, his thoughts and feelings as something separate from the rest - a kind of optical delusion of his consciousness. This delusion is a kind of prison for us, restricting us to our personal desires and affection for a few persons nearest to us. Our task must be to free ourselves from this prison by widening our circle of compassion to embrace all living creatures and the whole of nature in its beauty. Nobody can achieve this completely, but the striving for such achievement is in itself a part of the liberation and a foundation for inner security.'

Many of us fear what we perceive to be different from ourselves – the unknown. What an amazing world it would be if we could embrace the fact that we have more in common with each other than we think. We are all equal – race, gender, religious beliefs and social status are all illusions.

The beautiful façade of Huddersfield University displays a quote from Dr Maya Angelou: 'We are more alike, my friends, than we are unalike.'

The gorgeous Dalai Lama is a patriot for showing compassion to our fellow man: 'I have found that the greatest degree of inner tranquillity comes from the development of love and compassion. The more we care for the happiness of others, the greater our sense of wellbeing becomes.'

Compassion allows us to move beyond the illusion of separateness. When we open ourselves up emotionally, we can link with others and dissolve boundaries. In doing so, our soul is elevated.

One of the most beneficial things we can do for humanity is to show compassion to ourselves. How many of us are guilty of negative self-talk, or continually worrying about things we have no control over?

As you get a sense of love for yourself, you will begin to see the light in every person. Instead of quickly judging someone, try taking a moment to pause and see the person in that light.

An Angel is an expression of divine love. At its truest essence, it is purely the energy of love. The light that we share is also the essence of the Angels. You are a spark of divine essence.

Choose to see the world through the eyes of an Angel. Even when we feel at our worst, the Angels will see us as a light of hope.

When you look into someone's eyes, think, 'There is a light in there, and I am willing to see it.' Every time you decide to see the good in someone, you create space for that good to enter.

WHAT DOES IT TAKE TO BE SUCCESSFUL IN LIFE?

What success means to each of us is different. Success is ultimately about living your life happily in your own way, realising that life is a gift, and you are valuable. You are not in this world to live up to the expectations of others, nor should you feel that others are here to live up to yours. The goal should never be to create a perfect life but to live an amazingly imperfect life.

There are key factors that can help us to create a successful life. Continuous learning is vital to stay effective. Dedicate an hour a day to your chosen field, and in five years you will be the master of it. Good social skills can help you to succeed in life. Being able to build and maintain relationships is vital to making any progress in life, as anything you want will involve other people. People will forget what you say, but they will never forget how you made them feel.

I found this piece of advice enormously helpful when I started public speaking. I realised that the words I spoke were of relatively little importance in comparison to the passion and sincerity behind the words. Knowing this helped me relax a lot, and put me in a better position to talk from the heart and not the mind.

To be successful in life requires getting your mind to be certain that you can make something happen, and that somehow you will figure out a way. Have confidence that the Universe would not have given you an idea without the means to make it happen. Success is no accident. Living an incredible life is no accident. You have to do it on purpose. It starts by knowing exactly what it is that you want to achieve.

Getting into the habit of writing your goals every day is essential as they set your direction; clarity is power. Knowing why you want to achieve something will galvanise you to take the action needed to make things happen. Know what kind of person you need to become to make it happen and then programme your mind to make it so. Visualise what it will feel like once you've achieved your goals and feel the emotion of that. The final ultimate success formula is to notice what you are getting and change your approach if necessary. Remember: J.K. Rowling, the author of Harry Potter, was rejected twelve times before getting published. Do not give up.

TIPS TO BE MORE ENERGISED

To be more energised every day, protect your energy. Avoid draining people, depressing news, and anything that brings you down.

Be clear on how much time you need to sleep, and make sure you get it. Disconnect from electronic devices before bed, so make a point of not checking social media at least an hour before sleep, and switch your devices to aeroplane mode.

Generate energy by moving your body. Oversleeping and leading a sedentary life just makes you more tired. Those that take regular exercise have far more energy to get through the day. Find a form of exercise that you enjoy. It could be anything from swimming, Zumba or ballroom dancing to running. Get your body moving and feel more alive as a result.

Find someone that motivates you that puts you in a high-performance state, such as Tony Robbins. He uses high energy music at his seminars to keep people feeling engaged and in a higher vibration. Your success is even more guaranteed if you can partner up with a buddy that will train with you, but if not, there are plenty of inspirational motivational people ready and willing to help you on YouTube.

Hydrate and fuel yourself with proper nutrition. If the food you're eating is lacking in nutrients, you'll still feel hungry. That's why you don't feel full for long after eating junk food. Tiredness and headaches are often a sign of dehydration. Most of us don't realise that, when you're thirsty, you're already seriously dehydrated. Often, the body cannot tell the difference between being thirsty and hungry. A lot of weight gain can be avoided by simply drinking a glass of water half an hour before eating a meal. Aim to drink two litres of water a day.

Use words that empower you. Being in a negative frame of mind drains you. There will always be things to challenge you. Remember to breathe, and ask yourself, 'What is this situation here to teach me?' Create affirmations with powerful inspiring words and repeat these as mantras to centre yourself.

Gratitude puts you in a higher frequency. It will help you to feel better and more optimistic. Make it a daily practise to fill in a gratitude journal just before you go to sleep. List ten things, which could even include the clean water you get to drink, or the fresh air you get to breathe.

MANIFESTING AND ABUNDANCE

Manifesting requires asking for things to show up, and it requires you to be willing to be present. A beautiful quote from Christie Marie Sheldon is: 'If you pay attention consciously to what's going on inside you, on what you are thinking, you can change your world. With intention, you can change your environment.' We need to realise that we wouldn't be given desires without the ability to materialise them. If we have not done so, it's because we are holding resistance which is blocking us. Feelings of lack or unworthiness can block us. Fear of not having enough can block us.

Manifesting is the awareness that we get to create our reality based on our thoughts, our feelings, and our beliefs. In nature, we can see that every action has a reaction. This is essentially manifesting; everything is created on intention and feedback. Abundance means a lot more than having quantities of things; it means having things that fulfil you as well.

The concept of manifesting becomes a lot easier when we understand that, as divine sparks of Universal Consciousness, God, Source (or whatever name you would prefer), we are all far more powerful than we realise. We are living our lives on the cutting edge of creation, bringing into being whatever it is that we place our focus on. Our thoughts and feelings directly reflect the world around us. When we accept this power, we take responsibility for our thoughts and actions, and begin to behave from a place of abundance rather than from lack and fear. Remember, like attracts like, and it's what we feel that we attract. We're more naturally able to manifest when we're in line with our higher vibrational state of being.

The recordings of Abraham Hicks on YouTube highlight this wonderfully through the speaking of Esther. Abraham is a spirit who channels himself through Esther to reveal lessons in how the principles of the Universe work. He has coined the phrase 'The Vortex' – the state of being when we come into alignment with who we are as our highest being. This is the essence of Source energy with the highest vibration.

By training ourselves to align with this higher frequency, regardless of the unfavourable circumstances surrounding us, we can bring into our reality that which we truly desire. Everyone, of course, wants to feel good all of the time, but they don't know how. Life sideswipes us with setbacks, disappointment, suffering and tragedy. It's easy to react negatively. It takes discipline to stop resistance and practise the unconditional love of Source regardless, and then improve the circumstances we face.

When we're not clinging to resistance, the Law of Attraction will naturally pull us into the vortex. If we have a desire, the Universe can deliver it. The only reason it hasn't is because of the resistance we are feeling. By becoming a deliberate thinker - thinking on purpose and speaking on purpose - we can keep moving in the direction of what we want, and staying focused on what's desired rather than what's not. We become intentional rather than reactionary in our actions. Practising meditation and mindfulness helps us to step outside of the mind and observe, rather than react unconsciously to situations. Of course, we're still going to be affected by what's going on around us, but with a greater sense of perspective we're able to bounce back much quicker, enjoying a greater resilience and ability to cope.

It's worth realising that we can't stop someone from being mean by being mean ourselves. We can't help heal someone else by becoming unhealthy ourselves. We have to let go of what is, and keep the focus on what is wanted instead. As mentioned, it takes great practise to view the world in this way. As Albert Einstein said, 'No problem can be solved from the same level of consciousness that created it.' The first step to successful manifestation is visualisation. If you can see it, realise that it already exists – your job is to bring it into your reality.

We can make life much easier for ourselves by realising that life functions within a Be Do Have paradigm, as mentioned in *The Tree of Becoming* by Trevor Morris. This is also explained in the *Conversations with God* series with Neil Donald Walsh. Most people have this analogy backwards, imagining that first one must have things in order to do things, and be what they want to be. People believe that, if they have a thing, e.g. more time or money, then they can do a thing, e.g. buy a home, write a book, or have a relationship. Only then can they be what they want, such as happy, peaceful, content or in love.

We are all told that this is the way life works. Marketing has convinced us to spend our money to attain the feelings that we desire. But what we need to realise is that it's our feelings that create the world around us, not things. First, we need to be what we want to experience, then we can do what we want. Then, having what we want will come naturally as a by-product of this. By aligning with desirable feelings, we can let go of the ones that don't serve us. An essential part of manifesting is learning to create only those things that fulfil your deepest needs, and serve as tools to help you grow and have the best life possible.

Most people, however, think that having large sums of money will fill a need, allowing them to experience a feeling, quality, or situation that they currently don't have. This could be feelings of wellbeing, security, inner peace, power or freedom. They think that, by having money, they won't have to worry anymore, and they can take time to relax and not have to do things they don't want to do.

It's essential to understand that money and objects by themselves will not automatically fill your needs, or give you the feeling that you want. If you think that money will provide you with freedom, for example, you must find ways to experience freedom regardless. This way, you're no longer viewing money as something you create to fill a lack.

So, by following this, we can see that the fastest way to achieve mastery of living is to reverse the order of Have Do Be. We can understand that, in reality, the Universe works in the order that first, you must *be* the thing, e.g. content, happy, secure. Then, you must start *doing* things from this place of being-ness. Soon, what you are doing brings you the things that you've always wanted to *have*. The true formula is Be Do Have, not Have Do Be.

This creative process can be set into motion by looking at what it is that you want to have. Ask yourself what you think you would be if you had that, then immediately shift to being. Start there, rather than trying to get there. This is where the term 'fake it until you make it' arises, but rather than trying to trick yourself that you have something you don't, search for the appreciation for what you do have. If you want more money, think of all the ways you are already abundant in life. What would having more money give you that you don't have now? What deeper needs or desires would be satisfied? Now, think of a way that you can immediately start meeting that need with the essence of anything that will serve your higher good that is within your reach. If, for example, you think money will allow you to stop doing the things you don't enjoy, start letting go of the small things you don't enjoy right now. Perhaps you think money will bring you security; start developing qualities such as courage and trusting your inner guidance. We are all struggling in one way or another, but when we see problems as opportunities for growth and personal development, we will naturally prosper and thrive.

The person that decides to be happy has all the time they need to do what they need to do. Deciding ahead of time what you need to be can often produce that in your experience. 'To be, or not to be – that is the question,' as Shakespeare wrote. You may ask, 'Well, how can I be happy if I don't have what I need?' But happiness is who you are; it's already in you. You don't have to find these feelings from elsewhere; you only have to draw them out from yourself. You are the source of these things, not the seeker of them.

So, as explained, this isn't a situation of faking it until you make it. You must sincerely experience all the things that you are not currently feeling. The fastest way to make this happen for you is to cause another to feel it because of you. Causing another to experience what you want to experience makes you aware that you are the source, and not the seeker, of that experience. You must already have what you are wanting, or else you wouldn't have it to give. If you choose to be happy, cause another to be happy. If you want to be prosperous, cause another to prosper. If you wish to be loved, cause another to be loved. It's as simple and powerful as that. You will experience all the things you give away as you realise that you are the source. Life is designed to be a process of creation, not reaction. The only thing that stands in the way of us having everything we want are the barriers that we put in place.

When in some way we feel unworthy, undeserving, or perhaps scared of the consequences of our success, we sabotage ourselves, despite the current lack of fulfilment. Fear of change plays a big part in holding ourselves back from experiencing our fullest and richest lives. Taking the time to examine our beliefs to see if they serve us, and replacing those that don't with more positive abundant perspectives, is a highly beneficial practise.

When you look at something, the energy changes what you look at.

When you look at money with love, it acts like a magnet to bring you more money. Love the money you have. Give thanks that you have the money to pay your bills rather than resent having to pay them. By clearing away the barriers that have been programmed into you, it's then possible to use quantum physics to raise abundance levels. There are many common blocks. One is thinking you're a spiritual person and you don't need money. Another is the belief that rich people only care about money. You're also blocked if you think that you can't make money quickly.

As mentioned, when manifesting it helps to have the perspective that we are sparks of divinity. We are the eyes and ears of Divine Intelligence, and we have far more creative power than we realise. God, the Universe, or Divine Intelligence is all that is, and as we are expressions of that, we are not here to be tested, and there is nothing that we need to do. All things are possible, and our thoughts become the things and the events of our lives.

By becoming conscious of our thoughts and beliefs, we can ask ourselves if they truly serve us. We are in control of the thoughts we have that shape our world. By focusing only on what is desirable, we can harness the power of the Law of Attraction. Whatever we cause through our thinking is what we get back, nothing more, nothing less. What we think about all day is entirely responsible for what happens to us.

Through thoughts of scarcity, we attract scarcity. Know that all things are possible to those that believe. Create a life worth living for yourself by creating an image of how you imagine this life to be, then look at this image internally, as often as possible, and think positively about it. Visualise a short video in your mind of how you'd like things to be. Add as much detail as possible. As well as what you'd be doing, how would you be feeling? What would be the expressions on the faces of those around you? What conversations would you be having? What would you look like? Fill the vision with as much colour and life as possible and expand it as big as you can. Have the unshakable belief that this is what you will get. Now, focus as often as possible on this desired life, and look forward to it being fulfilled – it will soon belong to you. Where you put your emotion is what you will get. Think E-motion as being your energy. Monitor what you feel and what you constantly think about.

Henry Ford said, 'Whether you believe you can do it or you can't - you're right!'

Albert Einstein also said, 'Imagination is everything. It is the preview of life's coming attractions.'

Having a vision is everything when it comes to success. Everything that is seen comes from that which was not seen. The first aeroplane and the first operation for open-heart surgery are just two examples. Someone called them in. Conscious thinking is not the solution. It's our subconscious thinking that drives the outcomes.

How do we then close the gap between seeing something in the now and knowing it's possible to have it? We need to keep reaching for a better statement to tell ourselves: 'My life continues to improve, and abundance is out there for all of us. I love how the Universe will deliver to me exactly the same vibration frequency to what I am offering.'

If you want to create more abundance, then you need to focus on the abundance you already have within you. What areas of your life do you feel abundant? This could be the friends you have, your health or simply that you are breathing. This is a Law of Attraction universe, and what you feel will be brought to you.

If you feel like you want a relationship, instead of going looking for love somewhere else, look for love within yourself. As you pay more attention to your relationship with you, you will find that your cup overflows, and other people will want to be around you. The magic is inside of you.

You can't lead from behind. You need, as Abraham says, to be in the vortex, aligned with Source, eager with life, and releasing thoughts that hold you apart from that. Continually reach for the best feeling thought. Be a deliberate thinker. There is always a silver lining.

As sentient beings, we are feeling things all the time, with different people and places coming into our lives. Our reality is heart-based, not mind-based. Everything is energy, and everything is vibrating in constant motion. Manifesting needs to be brought back to feelings and ownership in what we are in the process of creating. Manifesting is the purpose of existence because we have to manifest to provide for ourselves.

Every emotion we feel is an opportunity to guide our energy in a particular direction. If we're feeling crappy, we can't reject those parts of ourselves because it creates resistance. It's a false belief that we have to be positive all the time. It's simply not possible. It's natural to have feelings of doubt and fear at times; it's part of being human. When people reject these parts of themselves, they block the intention from manifesting and appearing in their reality. Instead of looking at things as positive or negative, think in terms of being in the state of flow or resistance. This helps you ground yourself in the present moment and have power.

Being in the state of allowing requires releasing total control of when and how things show up. This is a joyful state, such as when you're meditating, or when you're happy and engaging in creative activities. This immersion in the present moment allows us to remember what we are grateful for.

It's important to realise that there is miracle in the uncertainty. When we're asking for help, by adding 'may this or something better show up,' we're making space for what we might not even have considered to show up. As mentioned, we can't always know how things will show up and when. The Universe can facilitate our profound spiritual awakening when we have an active faith that things will work out okay. Navigate the now with the assumption that you're going to be okay, no matter what. This diffuses the energy of resistance and allows the flow of infinite possibilities to manifest. When we hold on to the outcome so tightly, we block what we want from coming. Quite often, those that get pregnant, for example, are those that have given up trying. By peeling back the layers of resistance to get comfortable with what is, we allow miracles to unfold.

When we desire something specific, we imagine that we will be happy once this is delivered; however, to be satisfied with things just as they are is the secret to life. Media and marketing tell us that first, we need to have something to be happy, but this is not how the Universe works. As mentioned, first we need to be happy to be able to do things that make us happy, so that we can have the things that make us happy. When we are connected to our true self that's in alignment with universal love, life flows effortlessly in our favour.

So, own your energy and your emotions. Become aware of how you're feeling and be okay, no matter what shows up. Trust that you are loved and infinitely taken care of. Have a deep appreciation and gratitude behind the creative force behind everything. Have reverence that everything happens in Divine time. The good and the bad all serve a Divine purpose. There are so many ways we can work with the shadow side of humanity because when we resist it, we create more. When we judge, we become the energy we are judging. When we get our hearts and minds in the right position, anything is possible. We must give ourselves full permission to feel whatever we are feeling and trust that the universe is always looking after us.

If you don't have abundance, it's because you think that who you are is someone that struggles. If you're in a place where you feel lack, and you feel like you need something outside of yourself to fix a problem, then you need to shift your reality. Realise that you hold the power right now. You have abundance right now; you just don't believe it. Now is the time to change the situation and learn something new. You're going to learn things about yourself - about what you're capable of and what you should be doing - that you never imagined because you never stepped out of that door to explore it.

It's not about you getting that thing. It's about shifting into a higher vibration, a journey, the lessons you'll learn, moving into a new reality and being a happy person. When you let that energy of lack and desperation go, you'll naturally create a life worth living.

Sometimes, we have the belief that, if we're not enthusiastic enough about something, then it's not going to manifest. That's not the case. You can still set the intention for things to happen and then let that intention go. You don't have to keep focusing on it. Actually, by thinking of what you want in a low vibrational state, you're just muddling up the vibration. Let it go, and trust that your higher mind will work things out in the best possible way. Just keep focusing on raising your vibration. In doing so, you'll release your resistance, and everything will start to flow much more easily. You'll know if your thought is in alignment with your higher self based on how you feel. Your thoughts are the medium. But the ego must let go. If you could see the span of your life and what is possible, you wouldn't doubt it. But we do doubt because we're in it. Allow yourself to feel it, but at the same time, switch to a higher vibration. Do visualisations for five or ten minutes, but then let it go. Trust that the Universe will bring you what you need, when you need it. The ego's blueprint is not always the best possible way. Trust that, if things don't work out as expected, the Universe has something far better for you instead. As you do that, you start to believe in yourself more, and you begin to feel better about the whole process.

MANIFESTING TIPS

Place a small piece of citrine, the crystal used for manifesting abundance, in your wallet. You can also harness the power of Feng Shui and place citrine in the South West Corner - the wealth corner

- of your room. The money plant, or jade tree, is also a symbol of prosperity.

Having a green or red wallet is also said to be auspicious for attracting wealth. Using the moon cycles, where a new moon brings in new intentions, is also a powerful tool. Light a green candle and write your intentions down. The act of writing brings more power to the intent. Vision boards act as a powerful reminder to stay focused on what you want to achieve. You can also create a little video in your mind of you achieving your desire, filling it with as much colour and emotion as you can muster, and replaying it daily as a powerful tool.

Many people have successfully written themselves a cheque from the Universe for a set amount, only to be delighted that it manifested years down the line. This was true of actor and comedian Jim Carrey who wrote himself a cheque for $10 million for 'acting services rendered', post-dated it 10-years, and then kept it in his wallet.

In *How to be Your Own Genie*, Raleigh Valentine advocates finding eight river stones, painting them a shiny gold, and having them stacked up on your doorstep as an invitation to bring wealth to your door. The Chinese have lucky frogs with coins in their mouths. The truth is, you don't need any of these. These work if you believe that they work. It's your belief that is the determining factor.

I've been playing a fun game about money recently, having read about it in *Ask and it is Given, Learning to Manifest Your Desires* by Esther and Jerry Hicks. It's called the Prosperity Game. It works by imagining that, on the first day, you deposit £1000 into your bank account, then you have fun thinking about what you would like to purchase. The next day, it's £2000, and the following day £3000. So, if you played the game for a year, you would have spent more than £66 million. After a few weeks, you realise that it takes a high concentration to spend that much money. This means that your ability to imagine will expand tremendously. Most people don't use their imagination very much. By playing this game, you'll find yourself reaching for new ideas, and in time, you'll feel the expansion of your desires and expectation. In doing so, you'll benefit by shifting your point of attraction.

The Universe is responding to our vibrational offering, not our current state of being. If we're giving attention to our current state of being, then our future evolves much of the same. But, if we're giving our focused attention to these beautiful expanding ideas, the Universe responds to the vibrations of those thoughts. It is promised that joyfully playing the Prosperity Game will allow the things we want to flow into our experience. I certainly noticed a dramatic improvement in my reality since playing along.

Let's think about the miracle of letting go in the context of manifesting. When we let go of the control we think we have in this world, we actually allow the manifestation of our desires. You might think that the opposite is true – that you need to take control and work harder to get what you want. But in reality that doesn't work. In fact, it isn't until we let go and trust that the Universe will support us, that things will work out as they should.

There is a trick to this, and there are steps to take. First of all, your conscious mind will play its part. This is where you will focus on your intentions. Focus on what you want to manifest. This is where you will consciously focus your mind to feel that you already have what you want. What difference would it make to your life? How would you behave? Embody that person now.

Then, the next step is letting go of expectations, doubts, and thoughts of how you will manifest what you want. Your part of consciously thinking about it is done. Now, it is time for your subconscious mind to do the heavy lifting. It's impossible for the conscious mind to solve such complex problems on its own, but the subconscious mind can work on these problems effortlessly in the background.

Think of a time when you almost had the answer on the tip of your tongue. Then you gave up, and as if by lightning, the answer came to you. It wasn't until you let go, and let your subconscious mind take over, that you were ready to figure out the solution. This works for the most complex of problems and goals that we set. Let the subconscious mind to do the work. When it has found a solution, it will bring this awareness to your conscious mind, just like a lightning bolt.

This brings us to the final step. Take action. You can have all the information in the world, but if you don't take action, that information is useless. Yes, this part takes courage, but if you can take the leap of faith and trust in yourself, you will see miracles happen. You will be amazed at how this works. You will realise one day that you are living the visualisations you had in your mind. You will realise that you have manifested your desires.

MEDITATION TO MANIFEST WHAT YOU DESIRE

Take a deep breath in, let it out and just relax. Continue to focus on your breathing as you take another deep breath in. Breathe deeply into your stomach, and breath out. Letting go of all the worries of the day. There's nothing you need to do right now in this moment, so just relax. This time is for you.

Just let go of all the thoughts that are coming into your mind; let them wash away. With every breath that you take. As you breathe in, and breathe out. Washing away any outside thoughts. Breathe in cool, calming air, and breathe out the hot air that is of no use to you anymore. Letting go of stress, letting go of thoughts, just focus on your breathing.

Now, I want you to direct your focus onto what you want. It is now the time to consciously think about what you want. Be specific. What do you want to manifest into your life? Visualise it in your mind right now. What do you see? See yourself having already manifested what you want.

Visualise right now what it looks like to already have what you want. What feelings do you have? Take a deep breath and fully experience that.

You have manifested what you want. How does this feel? Continue to feel this now in the moment. Enjoy the feelings now of already having what you want. Realise, in this moment, that you have truly manifested your desire.

Now, if you have not already done so, bring together both the visualisation and the feelings. What does it look and feel like, now that you have manifested what you want? Breathe, and take a moment to enjoy this and appreciate how wonderful life is.

Now, the next part. The key to manifesting is letting go. Just take your thoughts now away from what you want, relax, and just completely let go of these thoughts. Your conscious mind has done its work. Now, it's time to just breathe and let go. Just imagine now that you are at a beach, lying down and relaxing. The soothing warm sun is shining on every part of your body, filling up every cell that it's touching, with comforting warm energy.

Gather this energy and send this wonderful feeling back out into the world. Take a deep, relaxing breath, and as you're lying on that beach, become aware of the soft waves rising and falling. Notice as they are coming closer to where you lay, but you do not move and you do not worry. You continue to feel relaxed and comfortable. When the next wave arises, it washes over your body, taking away all the stress you've been feeling. Now, you feel more and more comfortable, relaxed and lighter, now that all the stress has been removed from your body.

You welcome the next soothing wave as it washes over you. Any worries that you had left are finally washed away. You now feel worry free. And just let it go completely, feeling even more relaxed, comfortable and even lighter. You are excited now for the next wave, and as it washes over your body, it takes with it all the doubts that you had in your mind and body, and you are now left with only confidence and courage as you continue to feel even more relaxed, comfortable and as light as a feather.

You are now letting go and letting your subconscious mind take over. When the time comes, you have the courage to take action, but not yet, not yet. Now, you just let go and free your mind. Just letting go because you trust yourself. You have faith, and know there's nothing to ever worry about. It is coming to you. There is no need to think about how. You just let go and receive it when you are ready. Just let go. Just let go. Just let go. Just let go.

Now, bring your awareness back into your body, back into the room. Feel the energy that connects your feet to the ground, and imagine that you have roots like a tree pushing deep down into the earth. Take a big deep breath in, and when you are ready, open your eyes.

Manifesting is deciding ahead of time what you want to bring into your life, and how you want to be. You create your world, so expect miracles!

AFFIRMATIONS FOR ARCHANGEL ORION

'Thank you, Archangel Orion, for helping me to make all my dreams come true.'

'Thank you, Archangel Orion, for helping me to manifest a life that I love.'

'Thank you, Archangel Orion, for showing me the big picture of the Universe.'

'Thank you, Archangel Orion, for assisting me in reaching my full potential.'

CHAPTER 11:
ARCHANGEL JEREMIEL

Realigning with Love

Super Powers	Delivers motivation and hopeful messages to those that are troubled and discouraged / Assists in conducting life reviews / Emotional healing / Forgiveness / Healing unhealed patterns
Name Translation	Mercy of God
Crystal	Selenite, Amethyst
Colour	Deep aubergine that appears black
Helping People	Gives hopeful visions and dreams, helps people learn from their mistakes, solve problems, pursue healing, seek a new direction and find encouragement.
Attributes	He inspires hope, releasing fears, worries and tension about the future.

Archangel Jeremiel's name means 'Mercy of God', and he only sees through the eyes of love. He can help us to have a positive outlook and attract a loving solution, bringing forgiveness to everyone involved. The book *A Course in Miracles* says, 'God does not forgive for He has never condemned.' In order for someone to commit a heinous crime, they must themselves feel an incredible sense of isolation and overwhelming pain. If they felt the reality that we are all connected and one consciousness, they wouldn't have been able to do what they did. Archangel Jeremiel gives us a higher level of spiritual understanding so that everyone is treated with respect and tender loving care.

FORGIVENESS

Emotional healing has its basis in forgiveness. Forgiveness is not about letting something go or condoning the behaviour. Instead, it is about realigning ourselves with love once more because we care enough about our self to not be damaged anymore. Archangel Jeremiel can help us understand the miracle of forgiveness. He can help us move beyond stories of our past that may have been painful, challenging and overwhelming. He carries a torch of light, which is the light of forgiveness. By choosing forgiveness, we make the decision to take back our power that has been taken away from us. We cannot change the past, but we have the power to decide how to live our future.

We often avoid forgiveness because we do not like the idea of letting ourselves or someone else get away with something that has caused us pain. But this is not what forgiveness is about. Forgiveness encourages us to step out of victim mentality and empower ourselves with our own story and energy. It should be our priority to move back to happiness. We were not put on this planet to suffer. Archangel Jeremiel can lead us back to our true natural state of pure, unconditional love.

He can help you to review your life to date, so that you can understand what changes you need to make to realign yourself with love. There may be many ways that you're not showing yourself the love that you deserve. If your life is not exactly the way you want it, the time has come to take stock and redress the balance. What old beliefs are not serving you? What unhealthy habits are sabotaging your vision of being the person you want to be? Stay focused on the best version of you and you will become it. Joe Dispenza has some amazing advice on how to do this in his book *Becoming Supernatural*.

Sometimes, what appears to be a problem is a blessing in disguise. Always have faith that everything is working out perfectly for you, and put your trust in the Divine. Sometimes, the disappointment of not getting what we thought we wanted is actually just preparation for something far greater instead. In times of difficulty, call upon Archangel Jeremiel to help make the transition as smooth and harmonious as possible. When you think negative thoughts, you hold yourself vibrationally in opposition to what you want. Therefore, by deliberately choosing thoughts that feel good, you are aligning with your Source self. You're moving yourself into a better position where everything can start to flow for you.

That been said, as human beings, we are designed to recognise and fix problems. Negative thoughts can help motivate us to change.

Negative thoughts are a reflection of an emotion that needs to surface, and suppressing and denying these emotions only makes matters worse. These emotions then become repetitive and obsessive. Negative thoughts are designed to help alert us to something that we wish to avoid. This awareness then leads us in the direction of our purpose; moving towards what you want and need. It shows you how to more directly meet those wants or needs. Remember, those negative thoughts are a subjective perspective and may not necessarily be accurate; however, we mustn't be at their mercy.

Your number one job, as a human being, is to grow into the best version of you. Your success and results in life are in direct proportion to your habits; develop successful practises, including goal setting and visualisation, and take positive action to be effective. You become what you believe.

Don't be driven by what other people want you to do; instead, be driven by what you feel is the next right move for you. Everything begins with a thought. Turn your wounds into your wisdom. Failure can be seen as a chance for realignment; a chance to move back in the right direction. Your true passion should feel so natural to you that it feels like breathing. Live out the most authentic, highest expression of yourself. Get that vision.

When you're having difficulty interacting with others, be aware that people put you in a position to feel what they are feeling; this is their reaction to how you make them feel. This mirroring of feelings can be very painful if things are negative. Now that you are feeling how they do, you can address this by making them feel the exact opposite.

KARMA

When I'm conducting a life review and writing a personal numerology report, working on someone's karma is always an interesting section. We have come to believe in the West that 'What goes around comes around,' and that 'Karma will come back to bite you.' The term Karma comes from the ancient Sanskrit language meaning to perform a deed or action. This includes all actions that we do through our body, our words and our mind. However, the most important thing to understand about karma is that it is not some divine universal punishment or retribution process. There is no external judgement from the Universe over what is right or wrong. It is merely a term used to describe the cycle of cause and effect. So, in this way, we can understand that it is only a consequence of our inner intent, but this is likely to be something we're not even aware of.

The theory of Karma implies that, what happens to a person, happens because they caused it with their actions. This then follows the idea that all events, including moral choices, are determined entirely by prior events. We do know that this is a Law of Attraction universe. Of course, no one would ever consciously wish bad things to happen to them. For example, no one would ever choose to develop cancer or be murdered. Therefore, other factors affect the life that we live. However, with higher awareness we can understand that there is no such thing as death, and that we continue to live at a higher vibration, returning again when we choose to start again.

On a soul level, before we come into this world, our soul meets with our guides and teachers to work out our soul's blueprint. We work out all the situations and scenarios that our soul will go through so that we have an agenda to discover certain aspects about our life as a human being. We will then select the circumstances we are born into that will support that discovery as a human.

I have witnessed those with degenerative diseases, unable to walk, speak or eat and requiring full-time care and medication in a care home. I'm not sure it's possible to truly comprehend the life lessons learned and shared with family. Their soul obviously experienced what it was like to have to rely completely on the care of others. Each family member in turn had their own life lesson to learn alongside that. It must take incredible courage to line up with such a long and turbulent existence.

This is a duality world, a contrasting environment, so we can only know something through the absence of it. So, in knowing what we don't want, we can also know what we do want. This knowing is what fuels our desire, telling the Universe what to become. It is usually the ones with the most challenging and difficult pasts that evolve to have a higher awareness of consciousness. If we are kept safe and cocooned, there is no reason to expand and grow. Some people live their life by default, allowing their subconscious patterns to play out the order of events.

In contrast, there are those that realise that we are the creators of our universe through our thoughts. The latter actively choose to have thoughts that support their happiness and wellbeing. By knowing this, we can understand why it's incredibly important that we become aware of our thoughts and our vibrational field. Holding onto anger, resentment, fear, playing the blame game, and sitting in judgement only leads to damaging ourselves. A fascinating example of this can be found in Louise Hay's book *You Can Heal Your Life* where she accredits diseases and physical issues to emotional imbalances within a person.

The concept of Karma plays an important part in many religions, such as Hinduism and Buddhism. It is a belief that, once you come into the nature of the True Self, no new karma will bind. After that, old karma continues to discharge until you attain final liberation; this is a process of self-realisation. We, as human beings, come into this life under the veil of forgetting our true essence and our connection to Source. When we realise that our connection to Source is essential to our development, we are then able to change our perception of reality. We no longer feel the pain of separation, loneliness and isolation that the 3D reality would typically present to us.

In Asia, Karma is symbolised as an endless knot. Endless knots symbolise interlinking cause and effect, a Karmic cycle that continues eternally. The endless knot is visible in the centre of the prayer wheel, and it is important to remember that man is a soul and has a body. The more humans realise their unity with Spirit, the less they can be dominated by matter. The soul is ever-free; it is deathless because it is also birth-less. It cannot be regimented by the stars. We can overcome any limitations because we have created them in the first place, and because we have spiritual resources which are not subject to planetary pressure. When we properly place our sense of identity, we leave behind compulsive patterns and subtle shackles of environmental law.

The theory of karma can be thought to be an extension to Newton's third law of action and reaction. This is where actions of any kind, including words, thoughts or feelings, and the totality of our existence, will eventually lead to a reaction. Putting this in simple terms, it means that the same type of energy is coming back to the one that caused it. It implies that absolutely nothing exists, which does not comply with the law of cause and effect.

In terms of spiritual development, Karma is all that a person has done, is doing, and will do. To reiterate, karma is not about punishment or reward, but instead makes a person responsible for their own life, and how they treat other people. All living people are responsible for their karma, their actions, and the effects of their actions. We are responsible for our own happiness and our own misery, and therefore we create our own Heaven or our own Hell. Good intent and good deeds contribute to good karma and future happiness, while bad intent and bad deeds contribute to bad karma and future suffering. We are the architects of our fate. Jesus said, 'We reap what we sow.' As I understand it, we attract what we are a vibrational match to, so what we give out is what we get back.

So, the term Karma can be understood as literally meaning action or doing. Any intentional action, whether mental, verbal or physical, is regarded as Karma. Generally speaking, all good and bad action constitutes Karma. In its ultimate sense, Karma means all moral and immoral volition. Involuntary, unintentional or unconscious actions, though technically deeds, do not constitute Karma, because volition, the most critical factor in determining Karma, is absent.

Karma, in the way that you've been thought to think of karma, does not exist. When we think of karma, we hear the saying 'what goes around comes around', and we think of divine retribution as punishment to those that have done us wrong. We've been taught that we carry baggage from previous lifetimes that we have to learn our lessons from. What actually happens is that, when we die, we re-immerse with Source energy – a positive vibration of everything that has been desired by life up until this point. When this happens, we are relieved of all the resistance that we have carried through in this lifetime. Understanding this, we realise that it does not make sense that we would drag passed penance with us from one life into the next.

When people talk about Karma, they're not understanding what it is that is creating their reality and their vibration. Instead of seeing their thoughts as powerful points of attraction, they're expecting their words and their actions to create their reality. When that falls short, they believe that they don't create their reality. Even though they want something, they decide that there is a higher power that decides what their fate should be. They think there must be a higher power that is doing things to them because this is not the life that they would have created for themselves. No one would deliberately give themselves cancer or lose a loved one in a car crash.

However, in this 3D reality, life is an exact reflection of our energetic vibration. Karma is a misunderstanding of the Law of Attraction. In fact, it's your thoughts and beliefs that create your reality. Whatever you are thinking creates a strong point of attraction in the physical dimension. Your thoughts come from your beliefs. If, for example, you grew up in a family that struggled for money and you heard the phrase 'money doesn't grow on trees', then this could become your belief. You could then go on to live a life without much money.

The concept of Karma originated in a country with a caste system where you could not change your life. For example, if you entered this life in a particular social circle, you remained in that circle for the rest of your life. You knew your place and understood that it never changed. This is an incredibly painful journey because children were lost through poverty, and hideous things occurred with that type of a caste placement. It makes it easier to cope with that kind of pain, to think that someone else created it for them. It is easier for them to believe that they are being punished for something they did in a past life than to accept that the hideous acts occurred for no reason. This thought process is where the concept of Karma came about.

When we are choosing the life we will be born into, and what we are likely to experience, we are selecting from a concept of wanting to widen our perception. We want to increase our expansion. It is this idea of perspective that links how we progress through lifetimes. It's not a choice made through punishment, but rather through your complete awareness, so that you can understand what it is like from all angles of one particular perspective. So, the idea of Karma as a punishment is very outdated, and doesn't reflect the reality that we, as Source, have total control. We get to decide what we will be in our later lives, no matter what we do in this life.

It's imperative to step out of the idea of outside forces doing things to us. It may be painful to accept, but through your thoughts, you have made yourself a match to everything in your life. That means that every experience, both positive and negative, were attracted to you by default. It's incredibly important that you are conscious of your daily thoughts. That you witness things that are happening to you, that you've said you would never create for yourself. You have to identify these thoughts if you are going to change them. Then, you'll see that you do have the freedom. There is nothing doing anything to you, and there is no judgement for your choices of thought. Then, you can understand the progression from one life to the next, and not be held back by the concept of Karma.

CONNECTING WITH YOUR HEART & RELEASING RESISTANCE

The more connected you are with your heart, the more connected you are with your truth, and the more connected you are with your soul. Connecting with your heart is an essential part of your spiritual progression because the heart bears the burden of all emotional trauma that you have experienced throughout your life. Releasing that trauma is the by-product of connecting with your heart, taking care of its needs and wants, and listening to it. We are in a relationship with our heart. Our heart is our best friend. More than that, it is our life partner. We must treat our relationship with our heart like we would treat a relationship with a significant other. We need to nurture the relationship and strengthen the connection.

Most of us have one area of our life that we excel in. It could be our health, or it could be the strength of our social circle and incredible network of supportive friends and family, for example. But what about those areas in life where we aren't so accomplished? We sometimes give ourselves a hard time when we fall short of success.

But when we realise that we go over and over the problem, we actually end up activating the vibration of that resistance, perpetuating that which we don't desire.

In reality, there are only two states: allowing or resistance. Often, when we enter a state of allowing, the resistance ends up going away. It's when we have a set idea of how things should be that we encounter problems and things don't work out the way we think they should. When we develop resistance and we feel negative emotion, our ego takes control.

If you're familiar with the teachings of Abraham Hicks, you will know that we have a much larger part of us at Source level, which is our higher self – our guidance system. Knowing this helps us understand that noticing resistance is a good thing because it lets us know we are not in alignment with our higher self. If we're feeling negative thoughts, that's our body telling us that this is out of alignment with who we are.

There's no point perpetuating what we don't want by ruminating things over and over. If you want things to change, the trick is to raise your vibration. It's actually counterproductive to focus on releasing resistance, as whatever you focus on will amplify.

Remember, your beliefs create your reality. A belief is a thought you keep thinking consistently. The key to creating the reality you want is shift your focus. If there's an area in your life that's lacking, focus on an area where you're already high vibration. In doing so, you'll find the old problems go away. As you raise your vibration, you begin to experience a reality that's equal to that high vibrational state.

So, when you think of releasing resistance, think of paying attention to your focus. What you begin to focus on consistently, you begin to build momentum on. If you find you're feeling resistance, and by that I mean anything that feels negative, let that be okay. Be grateful and thank yourself because you have caught yourself in the act. Let this awareness make you remember the larger consciousness part of yourself - the Source energy and guidance system of who you are - and the misalignment you have with it as you over-identify with the ego. Your guidance system is just reminding you that you are so much more.

The Angels want to inspire you to ditch the fear and love yourself on a deeper level. Change is never easy, even when it's self-empowering. Be warned that you will most likely experience resistance. The Angels are here to help you with this. Trust in the process of being uncomfortable with uncertainty, knowing that there is a safety net, even when you can't see it.

The secret is to move from rigidity to softness. Think about what is more powerful – water or rock? We are 75% water, and so is the planet. Visualise yourself as water. The more grasp you have, the more you hold on, the less control you have. To experience water, be softer, more flexible, more fluid. Have an openness and willingness to change your mind. Nothing stays the same in life, so learning to adjust well to change is imperative to our long-term wellbeing.

Take a moment now to consider what changes you would like to make in your life. Our Guardian Angels are always whispering guidance to us for our highest good. Ask Archangel Jeremiel to support you in having the courage and determination to make these changes. Also, take time to reflect on how far you have come. All too often, we don't give ourselves credit for the achievements we have made. You are unlikely to be the same person you were last week, let alone last year. If you could give your younger self advice based on what you know now, what would that be?

Life can, at times, be overwhelming and scary, especially when we are faced with so much choice. An amazing way to take the fear out of knowing what to do for the best is to experience a Future Life Progression session. This is something that I offer via web link to guide people five and ten years into the future to see what they will be doing, where they will be living, and who they will be with. Wouldn't it be amazing to know where to invest your energy and focus for your maximum benefit, and avoid situations that weren't going to work out for you! Hindsight is a powerful tool that can get you on track for living the life that you desire. For more information, visit www.AngelicEnergies.co.uk.

AFFIRMATIONS FOR ARCHANGEL JEREMIEL

'Thank you, Archangel Jeremiel, for helping me to notice life patterns that are not serving me and giving me the courage to take steps to release those patterns.'

'Thank you, Archangel Jeremiel, for helping me see how the lessons I've learned are valuable assets for today and tomorrow.'

'Thank you, Archangel Jeremiel, for helping me to feel compassion so that I can see others' point of view and allow my heart to heal.'

'Thank you, Archangel Jeremiel, for guiding me to treat myself and others with respect and tender loving care.'

Guided By Angels

CHAPTER 12:
ARCHANGEL JOPHIEL

Enchantment and Beauty

Super Powers	Optimism / Self-esteem / Feng Shui / Enchantment / Beauty
Name Translation	The Beauty of God
Crystal	Ametrine, Smokey Quartz, Rutilated Quartz, Rose Quartz, Pink Tourmaline, Rubellite
Colour	Deep pink and golden yellow
Helping People	Archangel of artists, craftspeople and anyone creative from inventors, fashion and jewellery designers, architects, hairdressers to cake decorators, film makers and photographers.
Ray	2nd Yellow Ray of illumination and wisdom

Archangel Jophiel means 'The Beauty of God', and her mission is to bring beauty to every aspect of life, including the way we think and feel, as well as our environment and personal self. It's thought that

Archangel Jophiel was the Angel that appeared in the Garden of Eden.

When we're struggling with our self-esteem and need help to feel good about ourselves, or to feel positive about the future, Archangel Jophiel can be of assistance. She helps us to develop a fresh approach to life, bringing positive and optimistic attitudes, enhancements and pleasure. She can help us see the beauty of the world. She can help us have more appreciation for all the incredible things that are happening here on the planet.

She can be of service whenever we need a boost in how we feel about ourselves, our life and the world. She can help us to quickly shift to a positive mindset, clean up our space, and beautify any part of our life, including picking out the perfect outfit. All of us, at some point, have had a low opinion of how we look and have needed help in getting back to feeling our best.

Archangel Jophiel can help us see ourselves in a more loving light. She can also help us step into the space of self-care and recognise our own self-worth. She can help us feel self-love, acknowledging gifts and traits that we might not have previously appreciated about ourselves. When we can recognise ourselves for the magnificence of creation that we are, we can truly experience the joy of living.

Jophiel can help lift our spirits as we release the small things that have stopped us from feeling joy. She is the Archangel of optimism, which helps us develop a sunny outlook and attitude. She can boost our self-esteem, helping us understand that we have something valuable to offer to others. Archangel Jophiel helps us acknowledge our beautiful traits, both inside and out.

Archangel Jophiel is associated with the colour deep pink. The crystals tourmaline or rubellite are perfect for connecting to with her. She comes in on the yellow 2nd ray linked to illumination and wisdom.

SHIFTING INTO JOY

You must decide to be happy now, not tomorrow. Decide to be happy now, not when the money comes in, or when you meet that person, get a better job, or recover from an illness – now. Remember, the most precious resource you have is time. You can get more things, more money, but you have a limited number of minutes per lifetime. You can't afford to waste time. It's easy to take life too seriously. Relax and enjoy it more. Your happiness is not dependent on when your problem is solved, or your debt is paid or when that person shows you love. Decide to be happy regardless of your current circumstances. Decide to be grateful for the things you already have and be joyful. Shift the energy. Keep your happiness in your own hands, instead of being at the mercy of other people and events.

My first long term relationship started when I was aged 18 and it lasted ten years. I was blissfully happy for the first three years, swept up in the honeymoon phase of endorphins and all the feel-good chemicals new love provides. The last five years were an emotional struggle, as my independent partner went off to do his own thing in hobbies and working away. I had relied on being with him for my happiness. I gradually learned to do things on my own that made me happy. Even little things such as taking myself off to the cinema felt like a massive breakthrough, but eventually, the lack of communication broke down the relationship. It was a hard lesson to learn that no one else was responsible for my happiness. Since then, I've become much more independent in ensuring that I follow my path of happiness.

So, fill your heart with gratitude, and it will overflow with joy. You will experience the fullness of life. Throughout our life, we all experience situations, people, events and relationships that diminish our light. The trick is to learn to regain our power of self-worth by viewing these challenges as opportunities to grow. It's these moments of contrast that provide us with the desire to experience something better.

BUILDING SELF-ESTEEM

In every situation, we have the power to choose how we will react and feel. In some way or other, most of us have the limiting belief, 'I am not good enough.' Most of our issues come down to not loving the self. We criticise ourselves and measure ourselves against others, usually falling short and going on to suffer self-hatred and guilt.

Self-approval, self-acceptance and self-compassion are the keys to positive changes. Our beliefs make our reality. What you are choosing to believe, think and say will create the next moment, and the next day, and the next month, and the following year. Remember, you are the only person who can think thoughts in your mind. Realise that, if you are having negative thoughts about yourself, you are inhibiting yourself. You are unable to be yourself without reserve because you are afraid of your own disapproval and the disapproval of others. The voice of self-criticism has grown far too loud. You are hurting yourself. You are labouring under the misconception that you are not good enough, and if you punish yourself enough you will be good. The voice that hurts you is trying to keep you good so that you will be loved. It is trying to help you. But in trying to help you, it is hurting you instead. Now is the time to be compassionate, forgiving and patient with yourself. Now is the time to find approval for you.

There is a special Angel that we can call on to help us. Archangel Jophiel, the beauty of God, is there to help us lift our thoughts and adopt an optimistic, positive outlook. She can help us to be kind to ourselves and to begin to love and approve of ourselves. That's what we all need to be able to express ourselves to our highest potential.

The point of life is expansion, which can only ever occur from a place of openness and acceptance. Our natural state is one of love, and we exist to be loved and to pursue happiness. When you acknowledge that you are bathed in the highest frequency of pure unconditional love, and connected to Source energy, you realise that you are living in Heaven. You don't need to find love – you are love! The daily dramas that perpetuate the pathway of fear dissolve once you have this understanding. By choosing to live life in the highest vibration of love, you automatically connect to receive downloads of brilliant ideas and guidance to help in everyday life. Suddenly, life begins to flow. In choosing to focus on love, you are creating real, meaningful and lasting blessings for yourself and others.

The reality is that there are only ever two predominant driving forces for any of our actions. They either arrive from a place of love or fear. Choices we make out of fear can never be the right ones, and they will always cause us to suffer. There will never be any regrets from actions made from a place of love. Always greet any confrontation with a response of love.

Happiness, peace and fulfilment will seam illusive if you are seeking them in external factors. In reality, externals are mirages with hollow energy. Nothing external leads to internal happiness. See only love in yourself and others, just as the Angels do, and the world will reflect more joy and happiness than you could ever imagine. This focus strengthens you beyond any form of human strength, and you heal others with your outlook. Like a warm hug, the higher self pathway of conscious living feels warm and comfortable, as lasting peace, happiness and fulfilment is already within you.

'A person who has good thoughts cannot ever be ugly. You can have a wonky nose and a crooked mouth and a double chin and stick-out teeth, but if you have good thoughts it will shine out of your face like sunbeams and you will always look lovely.' - The Twits, Roald Dahl

Think of the mind as being like a garden. We sow the seeds of new experiences, water them with positive affirmations, and pull out the weeds of negative thoughts that come up.

Try a little exercise. Stop for a minute to think about a person that you respect, admire or hold in high esteem. Be as specific as you can, listing all the reasons why you selected that person. Now, can you think of another person as well? What exactly is it that you respect and admire?

My immediate first choice was the Ascended Master Jesus. I find it remarkable that, two thousand years on, he is still the source of strength and compassion, and unwavering faith that provides a tremendous sense of comfort and support to billions of people. Oprah Winfrey is another source of inspiration for me. It's incredible that she has built herself up from a poor and abusive background to becoming the fantastic outspoken, loving and passionate person she is, spreading hope and upliftment to millions. If I'm allowed a third choice, it would be the force of nature that is Tony Robbins. His energy and passion are infectious, and he certainly transformed my life in his seminar 'Unleash the Power Within', as he has millions of others.

Now, think about the people that inspire you. I want to point out that the reason these people inspire you is because you have these qualities yourself. The world is a mirror. You are only able to see what is inside of you. Moreover, if a person doesn't want something, they will be unable to see the excellence of that thing. The recognition of excellence is completely dependent upon the desire of the observer. I encourage you now to raise your thoughts, and stay focused only on solutions and what gives you joy. Even when you are born without many of the attributes and advantages of your peers, by tapping into your inner voice and harnessing your uniqueness, you can achieve great things.

Just know that you belong in any room you enter.

Act like no one's telling you no.

THE ART OF MINIMALISM

As well as being the Angel of beauty, Jophiel is also known as the Feng Shui Angel. This ancient art concentrates on the harmonious flow of energy throughout our homes and workspaces. As we live in a commercial society, we're constantly encouraged to buy more and more. The art of minimalism is becoming increasingly popular to assist in simplifying life. This is about identifying what has value and makes you happy, then eliminating the extras. So, getting rid of the burden, the clutter and the stress. This starts with decluttering the home, but also goes onto changing your consumption habits, where you are being more mindful of what you're bringing into your home and life. You're also re-prioritising life and where you want to focus your time and energy.

Changing your lifestyle might seem a bit overwhelming and challenging, but a great tip is to be clear on your reasons why you want to do it. This could include any or all of the following: saving money; reducing your carbon footprint; creating more space; reducing the time you have to clean.

Another great tip is to not feel like you have to do it all at once. This process takes time, so it's better to take continual small steps every day. Think of it as a lifestyle change, rather than a project you have to finish. Start by sorting out your wallet or handbag, progress to your drawers, and so on, but save the sentimental items for last. That way you'll already be in the right mindset to deal with the more difficult items.

Be grateful for the abundance you already have, and override the short term satisfaction of buying more things with the appreciation of having more money, space and time instead. Surely, that's more valuable than anything money could buy?

MEDITATION TO CONNECT TO ARCHANGEL JOPHIEL

With your eyes closed, take a deep breath, and as you exhale, allow the tension to leave your body. Let your scalp and your forehead relax. Roll your shoulders back, straighten your spine, and feel a silver cord stretching you up from the crown of your head. Now, let your throat and your shoulders relax. Let your back and your abdomen and your pelvis relax. Let your breathing be at peace as you relax your legs and feet.

In this relaxed and comfortable position, we call upon Archangel Jophiel to be with you now. We ask her to help you recognise that, in the infinity of where you are, all is perfect, whole and complete.

Affirm to yourself in your own mind, 'The past has no power over me because I am willing to learn and change. I am willing to let go. I release. I let go. I release all tension. I release all fear. I release all anger. I release all guilt. I release all sadness. I let go of all old limitations. I realise that all my power is in this present moment. I let go, I am at peace. I am at peace with myself. I am at peace. I am at peace with myself. I am at peace with the process of life.

'I see the past as necessary to bring me to where I am today. Thank you, Archangel Jophiel, for boosting my self-esteem and helping me to feel optimistic about the future. I am thrilled to be in the middle of this adventure, for I know that I will never go through this particular experience again. I am willing to set myself free. All is well in my world. I am safe.'

When you're ready, take a deep breath, come back into the room, and open your eyes.

MIRROR WORK WITH ARCHANGEL JOPHIEL

Mirror work is a daily exercise you can link to the time you spend brushing your teeth at the end of the day. In this way, it should become a habit. Keeping a healthy mind is just as crucial as oral hygiene!

So, while you're standing in front of the mirror, thank Archangel Jophiel for being with you at that moment. Fill your heart with gratitude, love and happiness. See your reflection in the mirror and smile at yourself. Look deep into your eyes, and in your mind, say your name, and then, 'I am proud of you today for...' Now, think of three reasons you have to be proud of yourself today.

Continue to maintain eye contact with yourself. Say your name again and then, 'I forgive you for...' Find three things that you have been feeling guilty for, then let them go with total compassion for yourself.

Take another deep breath as you continue to keep this eye contact with your reflection. In your mind, repeat your name and, say 'I commit to yourself that...'

Finally, think of three things that you can do to support your future happiness now. Thank Archangel Jophiel for her support in keeping your thoughts in a beautiful, uplifting place.

Do this exercise for 60 days, and I guarantee your life will dramatically improve as a result of bolstering your self-esteem and self-compassion. It sounds like a simple exercise, but to start with, it can be incredibly uncomfortable and bring up lots of emotions. The act of looking into your own eyes and bearing witness to your own soul can seem alien.

If I were to offer you the car of your dreams, on the proviso that this would be the only car you would have for your whole life, how would you treat that car? Your body is like that car, so be sure to treat it with care. Become your own best friend and learn to enjoy your own company.

AFFIRMATIONS FOR ARCHANGEL JOPHIEL

'Thank you, Archangel Jophiel, for helping me to beautify my thoughts and my life.'

'Thank you, Archangel Jophiel, for helping me to always look my best, and to declutter my surroundings.'

'Thank you, Archangel Jophiel, for helping me to always have an optimistic viewpoint, and be a joy to be around.'

'Thank you, Archangel Jophiel, for filling up my heart with feelings of gratitude and enjoyment.'

This Scented Healing Mist has rose petals dancing with creamy ylang ylang and sweet orange, with a base of soft musky woods. Comforting and grounding, this is a perfect harmony between floral and musk.

CHAPTER 13:
ARCHANGEL RAGUEL

Harmony

Super Powers   Resolves arguments / Mediation /
Cooperation / Understanding / Order /
Harmony / Forgiveness

Name Translation   Friend of God

Crystal   Aquamarine, Angelite, Celestite, Blue Lace
Agate

Colour   Pale blue

Helping People   Those fighting injustice. Motivates people to
support causes such as crime, poverty and
abuse. Guiding world leaders to make wise
decisions.

Attributes   He is the Archangel of justice, fairness and
harmony, inspiring others to act from
integrity, honour and truth, giving us faith in
humanity.

Archangel Raguel can help us see the bigger picture and take onboard everyone's point of view as he guides us to make the best decision for everyone involved. He can also help us see how our choices are going to affect others in the world. If you're troubled by an argument, need help resolving a misunderstanding, or want to make things go well among individuals or groups, Raguel is the right Archangel to call.

Archangel Raguel can assist us to understand our own identity, helping us to be aware and understand our feelings and to follow them. He can bring clarity and confidence to anyone who is experiencing challenges, guiding them to understand and accept themselves for who they truly are.

His name means 'Friend of God', and he motivates people to act from a noble, generous and benevolent place, supporting worthy causes. He also assists us in standing up to injustice so that we can resolve any conflict. Raguel also makes sure the Archangels and Angels are working in harmony and cooperation. He is associated with the colour light blue. So, wearing or holding aquamarine or another light blue stone will help align with his kind energy.

Archangel Raguel's primary function is to facilitate harmony and order in relationships. He has the power to resolve disputes and find creative resolutions that benefit everyone involved. Archangel Raguel can help us make friends, make up with friends, and help build bridges when we feel they have burnt.

He is also associated with justice, along with Archangel Zadkiel. He works alongside those who work in the legal world to assist them in bringing justice to the world. Archangel Raguel is brilliant in times of challenge and conflict.

VULNERABILITY

When we are made to feel shame, it goes deep into our primal needs where, to feel secure, we have to have a sense of belonging. In tribal times, when you didn't belong to a group, the chance of survival was very slim.

Regrettably, there is no such thing as the perfect upbringing or adult life. People get rejected, pushed away, and given an attitude of shame; we are all vulnerable and need approval for inclusion and safety. We all require a connection and belonging.

There is a tribe in Africa that understands this. When someone commits a crime or does something wrong, the rest of the tribe surround them in a circle. They then take turns to remind that person why they love them and what is good about them. This tradition integrates the individual back to the group, instead of amplifying the harmful behaviour in a detrimental way for them and the group.

We need to show compassion and understanding of the more profound need behind thoughts and actions. These thoughts and actions are just a cover for vulnerability. They are a sign that a person is not feeling wanted, needed or valued. We should remember that adverse actions are only ever done because a person wants to feel better. Every crime committed is done to try and escape from feeling vulnerable.

If we punish with isolation, we are making the individual who has done wrong far more damaged and dangerous as a result. It breaks my heart to hear of isolation booths being used in schools. When a child or an adult is put in isolation, they're not in there thinking of ways they can adapt their behaviour to conform. The pain they are feeling is merely amplified; they are looking for ways to lash out so that others can feel their pain and understand what they are going through. It is better to help people cope with vulnerability and meet their needs directly in ways that benefit them and everyone around them. We all have talents and skills that can be utilised to gain connection and belonging in society. If we can unearth these needs, they can be taken care of and resolved. For humanity's sake, we need to show compassion and understanding of the need beneath the initial behaviour.

COPING WITH CONFRONTATION

As long as human beings are going to be imperfect, then relationships are going to have some level of dysfunction to them. It's unrealistic to think that any relationship is going to be perfect at all times. In parenting, relationship dynamics change over time. The parent takes care of the child, and when the child becomes an adult, the relationship needs to change; no one has instructions for how relationships change. For so many reasons, we experience confrontation in our relationships; what we say, what we do, and what we don't say or do. Be consistent in your style of dealing with issues. Don't let others influence your response. How you choose to be is your choice.

Make a bold declaration on who you are and who you are becoming, and then be consistent. Don't ever ask permission to be you. How you are should not be monitored by people's response to you.

When something doesn't feel right in a relationship, you need to talk about it. If you don't know how to talk about it, the whole relationship stops. Not knowing how to communicate makes things hit the wall, and the ripple effect affects the relationships around you, too.

Confrontation stems from the source energy of 'I'm right, and you're wrong'. This energy is divisive. Communication is the key to every secure connection or every strong division. If someone makes you feel wrong repeatedly, you stop trusting them. Confrontation is more about you wanting to feel heard, rather than wanting to hear what was said.

Instead, have the intention to complete the conversation with the relationship still intact. That means maintaining the relationship becomes primary to what you're going to say. The problematic issues you need to work through still need to be addressed, just in a different way. State that you honour the relationship, but some things need to be cleaned up.

Don't be manipulative by saying something like, 'I like you, but...' Everything you say before the 'but' has no power or energy because everyone is waiting on the 'but'.

Neither can you start the conversation by launching straight into the problem. You need to deposit something into the bank first. You can't just start on empty.

Instead, honour and acknowledge the other person first. Say something like, '(Name), what I appreciate about you is...' and then list two things that you appreciate about them.

'(Name), what I respect most about you is... ' , '(Name), what I admire most about you is...' or '(Name), what I love most about you is...' Set the person up with what you like, love or admire or value about them, which raises them up.

Then make a genuine request for what you need support with; don't let it be about what they have made wrong. Say, 'I need your support in...' This might be difficult for your ego to cope with, but realise that, in stating you need support, any defensiveness will dismantle. Another way to state your case would be to say, 'What would work better for me is...' Alternatively, say, 'Can we make a new agreement to...' Asking permission ensures the person honours your request. Wait for a response. If they decide to support you, they will line up with that request.

If you dictate, they won't necessarily agree with you. If there's ever a breakdown, don't address the breakdown. Instead, address the fact that a commitment was made to you. So, you say, 'What I asked for was if you could agree that you would do... and you agreed to that. So, tell me, what should I have done differently?' This question confronts them with their own humanity. At that moment, you confront them with the quality of their own promise. The focal point is kept on the relationship being built up again.

RELEASING JUDGEMENT

It's easy to fall into patterns of behaviour of blaming, judging and shaming, but where does that leave us? It only serves to rob us of the wonderful, uplifting and magical life that's our birth right to have. When we give away our power to others, we allow their actions to rob us of our happiness and joy in life.

When we realise that our judgement is a reaction to a suppressed aspect of our self, we can identify what this is so that we can express it. Anything that we deny, object to or reject in this world is something that we've rejected about our self; it becomes a portion of our subconscious mind. Stop for a minute and think about something or someone that you have been judging. Now, stop and think about how they might be judging you in return. Take this to the worst-case scenario. Realise that this is what you've been rejecting about yourself and projecting onto them.

As an example, let's imagine Betty held the belief that Jason, who has a skinhead and tattoos, was someone to be scared of and was probably an ex-convict or addict. Now, how is Jason likely to be thinking of Betty in return? He is probably thinking, 'Who does she think she is? Why does she think that she's better than me? She's clearly very superficial – what a stuck up snob!' Deep down, Betty isn't owning up to the part of herself that tries to make herself feel better by believing she is superior. If she felt confident in her own skin, she wouldn't have the need to put others down who were comfortable in expressing themselves as they saw fit. Freedom comes when you bring awareness to your judgements of others.

So, why do we judge? The problem is that we've separated from love. When our sense of oneness is taken away from us, we feel separate and alone in the world, giving rise to fear to block the pain.

By judging others, we are projecting our pain onto them. In fact, it's because we feel inadequate or lonely. But the act of judging makes us feel subconsciously ashamed and guilty. In judging, all we're doing is redirecting our focus away from our own wounds. Somehow, feeling like a victim is safer than facing our own wounds. We're terrified of meeting our own pain.

What we have to realise is that judgement lowers our energy and vibration. We don't need to give up judgement altogether as it's instrumental in upholding our moral code. But all judgement is a disowned part of our shadow. It's important to honour our shadows. We have to realise that, when we judge, it's a call for help. We're looking to protect ourselves from not feeling loved. When we judge, we're just looking for love.

We can realise that we are all the same, feeling unworthy and abandoned when all we want is to feel free and loved. But the good news is that, any moment we judge, we can set ourselves free with forgiveness. We have the power to shine a light on our judgement and forgive ourselves for having a thought. In doing this, we shift our energy. Our health improves, our relationship with family, friends and co-workers improves, we eat better, we sleep better, and we become a better example for our children.

Ask yourself now, are you annoyed with someone? Does a specific situation irritate you, or have you got a grievance of some kind? Take a moment now to think about that person who is bothering you. Take a deep breath and close your eyes. Feel the energy around your heart expand. Now ask yourself:-

If I were behaving like the other person, why would I be doing so?

If I were behaving in this way, how would I feel in doing so?

And then:

How could I have created this situation?

How could I have drawn this grievance into my life?

What feelings does this situation create within me?

As soon as you have found something, you say to yourself:

I am sorry

I forgive me

I love you. In saying this, you are speaking to yourself here. You love both yourself and the feeling you discover within yourself.

AFFIRMATIONS FOR ARCHANGEL RAGUEL

'Thank you, Archangel Raguel, for harmonising all my relationships, healing all misunderstandings, and bringing forth forgiveness, peace and understanding.'

'Thank you, Archangel Raguel, for attracting wonderful friends into my life that treat me with respect and integrity.'

'Thank you, Archangel Raguel, for helping me distinguish between my feelings and those of others, and clearing any energies that I may absorb.'

'Thank you, Archangel Raguel, for helping me take note of repetitive emotions so that I can follow my feelings.'

CHAPTER 14:
ARCHANGEL CHAMUEL

Raise Confidence

Super Powers Anti-Anxiety / Self-love / Find items that are lost / Find important parts of our lives such as life purpose, a love relationship, a new job, supportive friendships and solutions to problems / Raise Confidence / Open up to new friendships / Heal strained existing relationships

Name Translation He Who Sees God

Crystal Rose Quartz, Fluorite (Pink, Green and Purple), Pink Tourmaline

Colour Pink and violet, pale green

Helping People Patron of surgeons, air traffic controllers, animal conservationist and those involved in peacekeeping missions.

Ray 3rd Pink Ray for the path of love

Archangel Chamuel comes in on the pink 3rd Ray. His name means 'The Eyes of God', or 'He who sees God'. He helps to open up our heart chakra, enabling us to see through the eyes of love. His gentle loving energy is the perfect anti-anxiety cure. As Chamuel is the Eyes of God, he is wonderful at being able to help you find anything you have been seeking. He can help you find lost items, your life purpose, a romantic relationship, a new job, and supportive friendships. He provides solutions to problems, passing on guidance through intuition. Chamuel has the amazing perception of being able to see the connection between everyone and everything. He also helps us to see the love within our self and others, and so connects us with our own self-love.

He is the Angel of the heart. His purpose is to see opportunities to love and expand our heart, as he removes the barriers around our hearts that stand in the way of us receiving love. He can help us see with our heart and focus from a loving state. Love is our true essence, and Chamuel can help us return to that.

'Your task is not to seek for love, but merely to seek and find all the barriers within yourself that you have built up against it.'- Rumi

Archangel Chamuel has a mission to bring peace to the world. He can help us to feel a sense of peace, protecting us from fear and lower negative energies. We can call upon Archangel Chamuel when we're struggling to find the strength and courage to face adversity. As he has a strong association with the heart, he can also help us with our sense of life purpose, giving us a love for life. He can help open us up to be more receptive to others, enjoy their company, and inspire friendships.

You can connect with Archangel Chamuel through crystals and colours associated with the heart chakra. These include pink rose quarts and green fluorite.

As 'The Eyes of God', Archangel Chamuel is the one to call upon to find anything in life, from a romantic relationship to a new job, or even your missing car keys or a parking space! If you need his help, remember that it is far more powerful to dedicate a prayer to state that help has already been given, rather than come from a begging or pleading stance. For example, 'Thank you, Archangel Chamuel, for helping me to find the love of my life.' You will notice that all the affirmations in this book have been written in this style because the present is the only place that holds any power.

ATTRACTING A PARTNER

When you are wanting to attract your potential partner, confidence is incredibly attractive. Know you are amazing, and anyone would be lucky to have you; be prepared to say why. It is also essential to make space in your life for someone else to be able to enter, mentally and physically. Empty out a draw in your bedroom and dedicate that to your future partner. Stop making your life so busy that you can't fit anyone else into your hectic schedule.

Do things that increase your chance of meeting someone. Put effort into engaging with others, perhaps online dating or joining social clubs or hobby groups. It's important that, when you're around others, your heart space is open and you engage with eye contact. It's far too easy for us to focus on our phone and miss quality social interaction. In having your heart space open, you're avoiding judging and analysing, and enjoying the connection instead.

Be open-minded because your perfect partner might not come packaged just as you might envisage. The important thing to focus on is knowing how you would like to be treated by that potential special other. Then, think about what type of life you want and visualise how you and your partner would fit into that.

It's important not to look for a relationship because you think it will complete you. Feeling that there is something lacking in your life will not bring the right energy to the relationship. First, get comfortable with being in your own skin and enjoying and appreciating your own company. Embrace this time to get to know yourself better, and boost your own self-confidence and self-esteem. Practise the art of self-love. You are probably very good at giving to others, but now is the time to give to yourself.

Finally, if you're interested in someone, have the confidence to let them know. Again, ask the Angels for help with this. 'Thank you, Angels, for helping me to clearly express my feelings towards...' The eyes are windows of the soul so let yours sparkle with the love in your heart that you have to share.

THE ART OF CONNECTING

Of course, meeting someone is only half the story. Making a relationship work requires being able to express your expectations and assumptions, as well as finding out what your partner's are, so that you can assess whether they align with yours. If you both hold the same values and are willing to support each other, you will be unstoppable together. Remember, you are never really alone. Your Angels and Guides are always with you, and they want nothing more than to see you happy, so call on them at any time for the support you need.

The more compassion we can show to our fellow human beings, the better this world will be. To show compassion, we have to have a level of understanding of what that individual is going through. In our day to day dealings with people, all too often we communicate to respond. This does not allow us to fully take on board what that person is trying to share with us. In our minds, we are too busy thinking about our own stories and how we can relate them back to the other person. Practise the art of truly listening. Try and feel the emotion in what is being related to you. Dispel judgement, and reach instead for understanding. We can never know the whole story of what is going on before us. Attempt to see things from a different perspective to your own.

How do we connect with another individual? We make sure that we are fully present with them by giving them our undivided attention. Maintaining eye contact is crucial, and a smile goes a long way to breaking down barriers. Most of the population feel socially uncomfortable in gatherings, so it might as well be you to break the ice. You will feel the wave of relief as the silence breaks, and the awkwardness dissolves. We all want to be noticed and feel a sense of connection. Perhaps on some level, we are aware of being of the same Source energy — the illusion of separation causes us more pain than anything else.

Be aware of the barriers to happiness that criticism creates. Those that criticise usually reserve the most criticism for themselves. Instead, aim to look for the good in situations and also with how you think of yourself. Instead of looking in the mirror and picking out flaws, appreciate the beauty of your soul, look into your eyes, and acknowledge that in every situation you are doing the best you can. When making decisions, take the time to connect to your heart. This is your moral compass, and it will always steer you in the right direction. When you speak from the heart, others will resonate with what you are saying as you will be living from a place of integrity and authenticity.

Loving Kindness Meditation

A beautiful thing to do is to practise the loving kindness meditation known as Metta. Imagine that your breath is coming and going from the heart. Become aware of yourself and focus on the feelings of peace, calm and tranquillity. Then, let these feelings grow into a sense of strength and confidence, and then develop that feeling into love within your heart. Imagine a golden light flooding your body. Then, go on to extend this feeling of wellbeing to a family member or a friend. Bring to mind as vividly as you can their good qualities, and feel your connection with them. Go on to visualise extending that feeling of positivity and connection to the entire human state. All relationships you have will benefit from you opening up your heart chakra, including the one with yourself.

Expanding your Heart Energy

Nobody is perfect, and it is painful to make mistakes. Emotional ties and disappointments can sometimes create barriers surrounding your heart energy, which will stop love coming into your heart. The Angels want you to know that it is safe to love and remind you that love is your natural state. May your heart be open and filled with love and compassion for those around, and for yourself.

Practise exuding warmth and love to people. We are all energy sensitive. When we practise exuding warmth and love, it becomes an invitation for people to connect with us.

Try this lovely exercise. As you're walking down the street, place your attention on one person. Pick out something that you like or love about that person. As you are witnessing what you appreciate, mentally say to yourself, 'I love you for...' Then, mentally say why you love them for that, and finish by saying, 'I love you for that.' As you say those words, imagine sending that energy out from your heart chakra towards them, as if sending that message as an invisible signal to their heart. Pick five people, and intensely feel that energy and emotion towards them. This will cause a ripple through human consciousness, and you will be amazed at how different your interactions will be as a result.

It's beautiful to hear of places of work starting up the random acts of kindness initiative too. Never underestimate the power that even the smallest of gestures have. We all have the power to change someone's life for the better just by treating them as our equal and acknowledging their worth. The world can sometimes feel like a cold and scary place. The more we can do to restore people's faith in humanity, the more it is reflected back to us. There is a beautiful saying that I try to live my life by: 'You must be the change you wish to see in the world.' - Mahatma Gandhi.

To help you attract more of what you want in your life, rather than what you don't, keep a gratitude journal. The Universe operates on a Law of Attraction basis. What you think about, both good and bad, will come into your reality, so it's all just a question of focus. Spend time with people you admire, and allow them to lift you so that you can adopt their attitudes and strategies. You can't hang out with negative people and expect to have a positive life. Consciously plan which opinions, attitudes and life philosophies you do and do not allow to be in your life. We become like the people that we expose ourselves to. You can accelerate your personal growth in whatever direction you desire by spending time with people who are already who you want to become. Release your fears to the Angels. Hold a vision of what you want, rather than where you are at the moment. As Albert Einstein said, 'Problems cannot be solved with the same mindset that created them.' The power of belief will open all doors for you, so be unwavering in your conviction.

INCREASING CONFIDENCE

One of the benefits of getting older is knowing yourself better and learning to care less what other people think of you. Having grown up as a painfully shy child, and being taught that children should be seen and not heard, I am now able to strike up a conversation with anyone I come across. We are social creatures, and quite often those that are less outgoing feel relieved that someone has been able to break the ice.

Everyone wants to be noticed in this world. Whether we realise it or not, we all crave attention. The simple act of acknowledgement to a fellow human being goes a long, long way. When you catch someone's eye, don't be afraid to give them a wave or a nod and a smile. Being in this state of openness allows synchronicities to flow. By being incredibly curious about others and life, we get to find out many interesting facts, most of which are surprisingly beneficial and relevant to our own lives. Having this approach is also a great way to start up supportive relationships, and even love relationships. Life feels so much richer with connections we make when we are open and receptive to others.

There are many ways you can increase your confidence. One such way is to acknowledge and celebrate your triumphs. This is essential for building future success. Keep focussing on improving yourself, and don't compare yourself to others. Posture plays a big part in how you feel, and by getting yourself to sit up straight, you will automatically feel better. Imagine a silver thread pulling you up from the crown of your head. Keep yourself physically fit and energetic, as a healthy body leads to a healthy mind. Stop feeling the need to apologise and start saying 'thank you' instead. Challenge yourself to do something new. When you break out of your comfort zone, you will feel more alive with a deeper appreciation for life and what you are capable of.

RELEASING ANXIETY

Archangel Chamuel is also considered the anti-anxiety cure. As love is the opposite to fear, invoking Archangel Chamuel in times of stress and anxiety is highly recommended.

Approximately 1 in 4 people in the UK and the world, as well as 50% of university students, will experience a mental health problem each year. In England, 1 in 6 people report experiencing a common mental health problem, such as anxiety and depression, in any given week, and those are just the cases that get reported. If you've not experienced anxiety yourself, you will no doubt know someone that has. As prevalent as anxiety is, it is not too difficult to treat. The preferred method through the NHS is CBT (Cognitive Behavioural Therapy). This focuses on changing the way we think about things, and putting in place coping strategies to break patterns of behaviour.

So, what is anxiety and how we can think of things from a mind-body-spirit perspective, as well as practical day to day things that we can do to help?

When we realise that we are a spiritual being having a human experience, we can appreciate that navigating our way through the dense physical environment of this world can feel tough. We can get so weighed down by the practical physical reality of life. Earth is considered to be a very tough training ground for the soul. Our automatic response to this pressure can be one of fear. Feelings of separation, insecurity, self-doubt, and being afraid of what other people think of us may surface. Anxiety arises when we allow our minds to focus on the 'what ifs' as the worst-case scenarios consume us. If we hold a rigid view of how things should be and wanting everything to be perfect, we set ourselves up for suffering. If we have not been taught to be flexible and adapt, or learn from failure, then we will not be able to cope with new and challenging situations. We will never put ourselves in a position to take a risk and follow what is truly in our heart.

Sadly, our brains are not designed to help us overcome anxiety. The brain is naturally wired to try and protect us from things that are scary, uncomfortable or difficult. This serves us well when we are doing practical things like crossing a road, or not leaving the house naked. When we need to be proactive, such as asking for a promotion or pay rise, we hesitate; our brain produces all manner of reasons why we can't achieve something. Fear has won and stopped us in our tracks.

When we become fearful, it initiates a physiological response in our survival instincts and the flight or fight response kicks in. Our digestive system shuts down, and our body focuses its energy on producing cortisol and adrenaline, which is designed to get you up and out of the way of danger. This was beneficial in ancient times when sabretooth tigers threatened us, but it serves very little purpose in our day to day living now. However, our brains are still hardwired to default to looking for problems and seeing the negative in situations. It takes effort to train the brain to function in a way that serves our best interest. But the wonderful thing is that the brain does what you tell it to do. By getting into the habit of telling the brain that this activity is something that you've chosen to do, and that you are delighted to do it, the panic receptors will shut down. By giving it positive commands to follow, you can break free from limiting beliefs. Here we're using the power of the prefrontal cortex - the part of the brain that analyses and rationalises - to stop the amygdala gland that produces the stress hormones.

Deep breathing is also very beneficial for mental calmness because it stimulates the vagus nerve, which runs from the neck to the abdomen and is in charge of turning off the fight-or-flight response.

Deep breathing also reduces the heart rate and blood pressure. The vagus nerve acts like a mediator between thinking and feeling as it listens to the way we breathe and sends signals to the brain and heart to respond accordingly. When we breathe slowly, the heart slows and we can relax. Conversely, when we breathe quickly, our heart speeds up, and we feel amped, or anxious. Try slowing the breath down by breathing in for the count of four and out for the count of six. After a few repetitions you can extend this to breathing in for the count of six and out for the count of eight.

There are, of course, times when worry can be beneficial. It can act as an alarm, signalling us to slow down when we rush into something unprepared, or when we face real danger. It's important to realise that fear isn't something to be avoided as it alerts us to a self-loving decision that needs to be made. In this world of duality, fear is one of our greatest allies in expansion; without it we would not know ourselves or Source. Ignoring or glossing over fear is not the same as looking at fear and choosing decisions based on self-love. We have to examine our emotions, including fear, and question them. Does your fear serve a purpose, or does it get the better of you? Negative patterns can quickly form if we are not mindful of our responses. Anxiety leads to more anxiety, which then leads to avoidance. If we are not careful, we talk ourselves out of what we first wanted, telling ourselves that we are not capable of achieving our goals. Avoidance only makes fear stronger.

I noticed this happening with my little girl. One of her best friends invited her to a dance class at the weekend. She loves to dance, but gets terrified at the thought of anything new. The screaming and tears we had at the start when she refused to go were incredibly painful. After dragging her along and easing her into it for the first few sessions, she now absolutely loves it. My son was just the same when joining the Beavers.

As adults, there are all sorts of ways people use avoidance techniques. Drugs, alcohol, self-harming, excessive exercise and sex, to name a few. Anything to distract us from the pain we are feeling.

It helps to have a broad perspective and remember that we have come into this existence to grow and evolve. In doing so, we continuously need to push ourselves past our comfort zones and embrace challenges. Allowing ourselves to be debilitated by anxiety robs us of our expansion and joy. In reality, the Universe wants us to succeed, and by calling on the Angels for help along the way, we can transform every situation as we realise our dreams. A Course in Miracles says that, 'If you knew who walked beside you, at all times, on this path that you have chosen, you could never experience fear or doubt again.'

It's also helpful to know that biologically the human body knows no difference between feelings of excitement and fear – they elicit the same response. Any high achiever will condition themselves to believe that they are excited so that they can move past the feelings of fear and get on and succeed in what they are doing. As mentioned, by telling yourself that you have chosen to do this and that you choose to feel great about it, you override the fear that holds you back. In any given moment, we have a choice in how we respond. By trusting that you can cope with different situations, you can learn to actively embrace discomfort and be willing to put up with hard times and uncertainty. Choosing a motivating goal helps to realise the potential benefit is worth taking the risk. There's a lovely quote from Teal Swan who says, 'If you'd like to fly, first you have to step outside of the cocoon.'

Attitude is critical here. Simply pushing yourself through a difficult situation in a white-knuckle fashion will not be of any benefit to you. There's no point adding punishment to fear. Remind yourself that you are motivated to do this, and that you actively welcome the discomfort that goes along with it. All performers get nervous before they go on stage, but they learn to expect the physiological changes in their body, and once they get going, the nerves disappear. When you stop being afraid of being afraid, and accept that it's going to happen, it removes another layer of fear. Remember, what we resist persists. The more you put yourself in uncomfortable situations, the more you prove to yourself that you can do it.

'Fall in love with uncertainty, and she will never cause you harm. Resist her, and you will be tossed and turned in her waters until you can no longer breathe.' - Teal Swan

When panic takes hold, externalise the worry. Here, the act of mindfulness is helpful as you can learn to step outside of your thoughts, rather than get swept along by them. Address worry for what it is and let it know that you are not going to let it get the better of you.

By shifting our concept of reality and raising our energetic vibration, we can go on to eradicate anxiety for good.

Living a spiritually aware life is hugely beneficial in overcoming anxiety. Our primary purpose in this lifetime is to remember that we are an immortal spiritual being having a human experience. We go through a veil of forgetfulness, so we forget our connection to Source, and that is painful. When we remember who we are, we realise that reality is what we make it. Life is what we see reflected back to us; we are a vibrational match. Quite literally, our thoughts and beliefs are creating our reality.

We begin to feel a sense of empowerment, which is the polar opposite of anxiety. The biggest thing we can do to combat anxiety is to practise the art of self-love. If you're feeling anxious, it's because you are a sensitive soul. In a world where many people have cut themselves off from feeling, being sensitive isn't a bad thing. Do everything you can to keep your vibration high.

Start by being deliberate about where you put your attention. Avoid news and films etc that make you feel as if life is happening to you. Instead, place your attention on what makes you feel empowered. Raise your vibration by listening to comedy and uplifting music.

Put yourself in a good state before you go to sleep, and when you wake up. Esther and Jerry Hicks call this 'putting yourself in the vortex'. Start a gratitude journal and practise conscious deep belly breathing. Stabilise your blood sugar levels, so avoid sugar, fried food, caffeine and alcohol. Stick to things like whole grains, dark chocolate, nuts and pumpkin seeds, vitamin B6 and B12, and drink chamomile tea.

Form social connections, as isolation increases feelings of anxiety. Get plenty of sleep. You are a multidimensional being. Most of our energy exists outside of our body. When we sleep, we are no longer constricted by our limited five senses, and we connect back with different dimensions as our higher self. Also, when you fall asleep, you are realigning. Daily, you are releasing all the resistance that you carry with you.

Enjoy meditation, relaxation techniques, yoga, Qi Gun. When cortisol levels build up, it helps to find healthy ways to release it through exercise, deep breathing and writing about the stressful thoughts. Drinking plenty of filtered water is also recommended, as the water helps the liver get rid of excess hormones, including cortisol.

If anxiety has stopped you from doing something, then get very clear about all the reasons why you had that desire to do it in the first place. Be reassured in the fact that you would not have been given an idea without the ability to make it come true. Next, remember all the times in your life where you have been successful at something. What challenges in your past have you overcome?

Expect worry to show up and, when it does, externalise the feelings so that you can observe what is happening, and not allow fear and worry to take over the show. Realise it's ok to get nervous, but know that you will get through this. Be willing to not know how things will turn out, and put your faith in the Angels and divine timing. Be prepared to feel physically uncomfortable, safe in the knowledge that your higher self is revealing to you what you need to feel completely fulfilled.

Affirmations for Archangel Chamuel

'Thank you, Archangel Chamuel, for helping me to find what I have misplaced.'

'Thank you, Archangel Chamuel, for ensuring that all my relationships are harmonious.'

'Thank you, Archangel Chamuel, for helping me to love meeting new people while I enjoy a great social life.'

'Thank you, Archangel Chamuel, for helping me find my life purpose/better job/home/relationship.'

This Scented Healing Mist has a sweet cinnamon that brings warmth and comfort. It is balanced in harmony with blonde woods and pink pose to create a rich, velvet-like softness.

CHAPTER 15:
ARCHANGEL HANIEL

Intuition and psychic abilities

Super Powers Psychic and intuitive abilities / imagination / emotions / clairvoyance / sacred feminine energy / full moon cleansing energy / inner wisdom / vision to see divine gifts and qualities

Name Translation Grace of God or Joy of God

Crystal Moonstone

Colour Bluish white

Helping People Patron of feminine support.
Psychics.

Attributes Represented as a feminine figure associated with the moon and the planet Venus, her high energy vibration can help us with our intuition and clairvoyance.

If you'd like to become more intuitive and grow your spiritual gifts, then call upon Archangel Haniel for assistance. A wonderful way to receive guidance is through the oracle cards. There are so many beautiful decks available that provide amazing insight, comfort and guidance. Once you have found a deck that you like the look of, take your time to familiarise yourself with each card. Set the intention that readings will be given for the highest good. You can then thank Archangel Haniel and your team of spiritual support for guiding you to what you need to know. Archangel Haniel can help you give readings for others or for yourself. Archangel Haniel's name means 'Grace of God'. She can help us develop our sensitivity, seeing our sensitivity as a gift and not a curse as we learn to honour our feelings. The more we are able to tune in to how we feel and our own energy, the better we can pick up external energy that may wish to connect with us. With her powerful goddess connection to the moon, Archangel Haniel can be of great assistance with any issues to do with the menstrual cycle and the menopause.

She has a luminous light that can open up our third eye to assist us in seeing our divine gifts and spiritual qualities more clearly. As we become more aware, it's likely that we begin to see symbols of feathers, repeated numbers and pennies, as well as other things. These all let us know we are on the right track, and the Universe is supporting us.

If you own crystals, include Haniel in cleansing them during the full moon. She can also cleanse all healing tools, including tarot and oracle cards, to aid in increased intuitive abilities. It is very beneficial to charge a moonstone crystal under the full moon and then wear it at times relating to your menstrual cycle.

As the moon governs Archangel Haniel and the sun governs Archangel Uriel, they work well together to balance the polarities within us. Call upon them both for assistance with chemical imbalances such as bipolar disorder, jet lag and Seasonal Affective Disorder (SAD).

Harnessing the cycles of the moon is helpful for powerful emotional release and manifestation rituals. This New Moon ritual was taught to me by Donna Campbell-Humphrey, and it was given to her by her guide. Donna runs Float-ology and the festival Imaginatix in Huddersfield.

New Moon Ritual

On the evening of a new moon, have with you a pen and paper, selenite to place on the third eye for mediation, a flower to represent things blossoming, then something to represent the four elements. Also include a piece of sage for smudging, a candle, a bowl of water, and moonstone (or other crystal).

Begin by giving thanks for everything you have in this lifetime and everything you have had in previous lives. Feel in your heart the gratitude you have for everything you are thankful for, and then light a piece of sage and smudge yourself.

Next, take a piece of paper and a pen and write down everything that you would like to bring into your life over the next cycle. Do not get too concerned about time.

The purpose of this exercise is to send out your intention and to trust that it has already happened.

To speed up the process of your desires coming to fruition, make a list of what needs to be done to make the things you want to happen.

When you have done that, write down what difference to your life and those around you it would make once these desires have manifested. How would you feel? What would happen in this perfect day? Truly feel into the emotion. Take the piece of paper, fold it up, and place a moonstone on top of it.

Now, lie down and place the selenite on your third eye. Ground yourself by connecting yourself from the base of your spine to the Earth Star deep below the ground. Feel the roots coming from your spine deep down into the ground. Connect the Chakra above your head up into heavens, so you are connected above and below. Remember everything that you have just written down. How does your perfect day look? How does it feel? Feel all of the emotions this perfect day would give you.

Now, disconnect from your Earthstar. Feel the roots pulling back inside of you. There is just a glow now at each end where you were connected.

Place the paper with the flower on a table along with the other elements. Think now how you can raise your energy in times when it may struggle, for example, with feelings of anger, jealousy, guilt, and shame. What would you do to be able to bring yourself up and out of those lower vibrations? What makes you instantly happy?

Let the request for what you desire go now, and trust that it has already happened.

You can perform a Full Moon ritual in the same way as the New Moon ritual. However, your focus should now be what you wish to release from your life, for example, emotions or beliefs that are no longer serving you. You can and should also release people that are no longer supporting you and your happiness.

Tips to Improve Your Intuition

A great way to strengthen your intuitive skills is through getting into the habit of spending five minutes every day to record predictions. Try and be as relaxed about this as possible, and avoid getting emotionally invested in what you are writing. What you write may seem like nonsense, but don't let that concern you. Your subconscious mind can communicate in symbols and shorthand with associations in ways you might not consciously understand. Let this be as lucid as possible without any conscious guesses based on present knowledge. The more you can let yourself go, the better the results will be.

Make a note of the day and time as you write your predictions, but don't worry about giving a predicted time unless you're given a date or time. Check back over your predictions and avoid stretching the meaning of any given prediction to try and make it fit. If you are successful, write down various aspects that apply to the event.

Also, make a note of every time you had a psychic nudge and were proved right. Perhaps you were just thinking of someone and you bumped into them that very same day. Maybe you had an urge to travel a different way home, only to discover that you avoided a bad traffic jam where there had been an accident. The more you pay attention to these occurrences, the more frequently they will occur.

Practise becoming aware of all of your senses. This can be done in meditation, where you sit and tune into everything that you can hear, everything you can see (with your eyes closed), what you can taste, what you can smell, and all the feelings you are currently experiencing through touch. Start with each one individually and then bring them into symphony together. This exercise can also be done with the eyes open while outside walking. Our intuition is our sixth sense, and this becomes stronger when our other senses are heightened.

Build your clairvoyance by practising the art of visualisation. Pick an everyday item, such as a piece of fruit, close your eyes, and try to picture it in your mind's eye. To become good at anything we simply need to practise. Intuition is just like a muscle. The more we use it and pay attention to it, the stronger it becomes.

MEDITATION TO IMPROVE YOUR INTUITION

Close your eyes and take a deep breath, and as you exhale, allow the tension to leave your body. As you connect to your breath, ensure your feet are firmly planted on the ground if you can. Allow your palms to face upwards, ready to receive, as you sit comfortably with your back straight and supported with your head free. Imagine a silver cord is pulling you up from the crown of your head.

Picture a pearly blue and white light surrounding you now as we call in the Archangel of divine communication through clear perception, Archangel Haniel, to reconnect us to our intuition. Feel this energy now, and know that you are being fully guided and supported by this process.

This beautiful light that you are surrounded by will only allow light to enter. All that is not light will be transformed into the light so that you can be the light that you were born to be. With Haniel's loving support, we ask that your sixth sense, which acts as your guidance system, be enhanced. We ask that you receive a boost to your psychic abilities, your clairvoyance and your intuition.

There may have been many times in your life where you were put in a position to have to go along with someone else's wishes instead of being able to follow your own inner voice. There may have been many times when you felt powerless, as your inner guidance was silenced. There may have been times when you yourself did not listen to your inner knowing, only to have regretted this decision. In this moment, you are invited to take your power back and let go of the fears of limitation. You are encouraged to fully trust your inner guidance.

Recognise that, as a spark of the Divine, it is your birth right to be a powerful being and feel supported. You deserve to live a life of abundance. To experience this birth right, you have to reclaim your power and remove any blocks that stand in the way of feeling your most connected self.

Archangel Haniel, thank you for standing with me at this moment.

Ascended masters and ancestral guides, thank you for holding me in light of protection.

Today, I am ready to remove from my energy field any old fears, limitations, stories, or anything else that has stood between me and my power.

At this moment, I am also willing to reclaim any power that I have given away, whether that be to people, places or situations. I call it back now.

In your mind's eye, imagine all the power that you gave away being returned to you now. Become aware of your energy field surrounding your body, breathe deeply and imagine that energy field glowing brighter and brighter. All the power that had been stripped away from you is now returning to you, and as you breathe deeply, you can feel yourself becoming stronger and stronger. This power is rightfully yours, and now is the time to celebrate who you truly are. With each inhale and with each exhale, feel more and more power, energy, prana, chi, returning to you. As this energy returns to you, may it fulfil you. May it heal you. May it restore any energy to you that you feel you may have lost. May it restore you of life force, wellness, goodness and greatness. Breathe. Receive. Have full confidence that your Angels and guides are with you in every moment. Their voice sounds just like your own, and it is continuously guiding you for your best wellbeing. Know that this voice is never criticising, never coming from a place of fear or judgement. Love guides you.

As you bask in Haniel's divine blue and pearl white light, say to yourself:-

'Today, I vow to take the time every day to sit in silence and meditate, and in making this connection with myself and the Divine,

I will continually strengthen my inner voice of intuition.

'Thank you, Archangel Haniel, for all your love and support.'

Breathing deeply, bring your awareness back into the here and now.

DIVINE FEMININE

The goddess aspect of Archangel Haniel represents the divine feminine. This energy represents creation, birth, life, healing, restoration, renewal, nurturing, love, compassion, intuition, connection, harmony and sensuality. Each of us has our unique expression of these energies that we need to allow to flow through us. We should be aware not to rebel against these expectations, or to the other extreme, embrace expectations that we don't enjoy to gain acceptance and approval. Resistance is disallowing who we are. It will only attract more of what we are resisting. Our actions should feel like they empower us. We should only commit to actions that add to our happiness. Find out what serves your happiness and what doesn't; this requires being very honest with yourself.

Sit and consider for a moment what it means to be female in your family? What does it mean to be female where you live? We all have different goals and the things that feel good to us differ.

It is not essential to wear high heels and dresses to be feminine, although you may feel more power and alignment when you do. However you choose to dress is your choice, as long as no negative emotions are felt towards how you don't present yourself.

Divine feminine energy is felt through the act of creation. There are no limits to the way that you could create. You may be drawn to dance, paint, crochet, collage, make jewellery or sculpture, for example.

Collaborate and come together with groups of women for healing, talking, baking, knitting. Other women can help you come into alignment with your divine feminine. I will never forget the incredibly supportive and nurturing energy of the baby yoga classes I attended after having my firstborn. At this time, I was physically and emotionally blown open; this gentle and allowing matriarchal energy was so comforting and strengthening.

Celebrate the beauty in your life. Do your surroundings reflect sensuality? Are they aesthetically pleasing to you? Treat yourself to flowers and make things feel soft and welcoming.

What is your relationship like with your mother? There is no such thing as the perfect parent, and usually limiting beliefs are passed on. It is essential to forgive to acquire peace within. Forgiveness does not mean you condone the actions taken against you. Forgiveness means that you love yourself enough not to let them affect you in this present moment.

Womanhood and feminine energy are a state of receptivity where we are in a state of profound openness. Logic does not rule feminine energy. Sink into your intuition, openness, compassion, love and gentleness towards yourself and the world; this is your true expression.

AFFIRMATIONS FOR ARCHANGEL HANIEL

'Thank you, Archangel Haniel, for bringing me polarity and balance.'

'Thank you, Archangel Haniel, for helping me to connect with my inner vision and wisdom.'

'Thank you, Archangel Haniel, for helping my gifts and talents to shine.'

'Thank you, Archangel Haniel, for helping me to harness my sacred feminine energy.'

CHAPTER 16:
ARCHANGEL RAZIEL

Connection to Divine Wisdom

Super Powers   Meditation / Psychic Gifts / Enlightenment / Channelling / Spiritual Growth / Brings natural gifts from you past lives into this life / Removes obstacles and blocks keeping you from your divine path.

Name Translation   Secret of God

Crystal   Clear Quartz

Colour   All the colours of the rainbow

Helping People   Patron Angel of Law Makers and Lawyers. Those wishing to connect to a higher truth. Integrate your shadow self. Integrates downloads of higher light and awareness.

Attributes   Angel of spiritual insight. The master magician and Angel of Alchemy.

Archangel Raziel's name means the 'The Secrets of God', and he is said to sit at the throne of God writing down all he hears. For this reason, he is the keeper of the Akashic Records – records that detail past lifetimes and soul contracts. Raziel can help us recall all the lessons that our soul has gathered across time to give us knowledge and understanding in this lifetime. Archangel Raziel assists us in opening up our third eye, unlocking our intuition and our natural capacity to be mediums. He can also help interpret your night-time dreams, as they represent the current vibrational condition of the dreamer. He helps us unlock our spiritual gifts so that we can set upon the truest potential of our spiritual path.

The Angel of Mysteries, Archangel Raziel is a wizard able to help understanding esoteric knowledge and turn it into wisdom. His reality is the full knowledge of God and of the Universe. Archangel Raziel helps us to master the secrets of spiritual growth and universal laws, seeing underlying patterns in life, along with new opportunities, time tracks and possibilities. He is able to align our body, mind and soul as one, as well as helping us to channel our spiritual gifts. He guides those that seek the secrets of spiritual enlightenment, opening up their subtle sensitivity and psychic abilities so they can more fully understand the deeper significance of life and the secrets of the Universe. Raziel is associated with all the colours of the rainbow, and you can use clear quartz to connect to him.

ENLIGHTENMENT

What does it mean to be spiritually aware? Many of us, myself included, class themselves as being spiritual and not religious. We have woken up out of subconscious behaviour and realise that the world happens for us, not to us. We have realised that we can create our own reality. Everyday life on Earth exists in a three dimensional reality of duality, where we can only know something through the absence of it. Here, fear, greed, power, jealousy, arrogance, envy, status and materialism are present because the ego makes us feel separate instead of connected. Information is sold for profit and recognition.

Being in the third dimension, we are ruled by the ego. The ego wants to measure everything and decide what is real and what is not. We come to Earth to learn duality. When we are identifying with our ego, we are caught up in duality. There is a polarisation of energy where we have to know one extreme to know another. The concept of war is a 3D reality – me versus you. Instead, realise that you are a reflection of me and at a greater level, we know that we are connected. Giving importance to the race and culture we came from - emphasising how different we are and judging what is bad and what is good - is a 3D idea. Fortunately, we are experiencing a significant shift as the energy of the planet is being raised.

Fear, shame and guilt are 3D states of consciousness. Neutrality is a powerful state as that's when we have the power to transform our self.

Fourth dimension reality is where you begin to realise that everything is not what it seems. We start to awaken to the reality that we are more than just our thoughts and just this body. We realise that we are higher spiritual beings living a temporary human experience. There is a shift to helping others achieve a positive reality alongside you. Information is shared freely. There is a lack of ego satisfaction and love is seen in all things. It is understood that individuals are collectively responsible for each other, striving for communal growth.

The fourth dimension is the dream state and time. Understanding that life is a dream makes it flexible and malleable. There is an idea of connection, but there is still a view of being caught up in good and bad. The fourth dimension is where we learn to change our beliefs; we understand that we can change our reality.

5D is the highest dimension you can shift to on Earth, where you are fully awakened. This is living with unconditional love, no matter what. Pure love, joy, peace, freedom, compassion and spiritual wisdom prevail. As you hold this higher vibration, you will start to attract people in the same vibration as you. Lower level states will simply not affect you. You will know and feel divinely guided by something higher than your own imagination. Synchronistic moments and signs will happen more and more frequently.

In a fifth dimensional state, we realise our own divinity. We exist in a state of love and connection with everything and everyone around us. As powerful creators of our own reality, we realise that this is an abundant universe; there is no need to feel scarcity or lack. We understand that if we hurt others, we are only hurting ourselves. We are filled with compassion and grace, feeling fully supported and in complete trust of the universal laws that govern us.

Fifth dimensional consciousness is about us connecting to our heart, to love and integration. There is an awareness that everything on the outside is a reflection of the inside. The mind is still polarised with the left brain for logic and right brain for intuition, however, the heart becomes the singular point of focus. When you create from the heart, you do not create from duality.

When you create from duality, it's a rocky path as you're thinking, 'I really want this, and if I don't have it then...' and there are expectations and rules. But if you create from the heart, there are no rules. You do it because it's part of the journey; you're not focused on the end destination. The ego wants the end destination only, but the fifth dimensional habit to adopt is to observe the 3D duality and let it be there. The more we focus on the resistance of it, the more resistance we create. Yes, conflict will exist, but by seeing it as it is, we lessen the charge that keeps us tied into the 3D reality.

We can learn to transcend these realities by becoming fully present within ourselves and facing what we thought was unacceptable as a child in our shadow self. We no longer disown parts of our self, so move into a place of alignment. There is no longer a fragmentation of the self where parts of us were rejected. We have faced the emotions that were difficult to handle, and treated ourselves with the compassion and understanding needed to heal. There is no judgement, no right or wrong, just a moral integrity that benefits everyone, not just the individual.

Spiritual progression is not about becoming happy all the time; it's about being willing to feel more. It's not that we feel better, it's so we get better at feeling.

Everything in this universe is energy. It is possible to rise and operate from a fifth dimensional perspective by deciding what frequency and vibration you want to run from regularly. Emotions and thoughts are the 3D operating system. Make a conscious choice to align with the energy of that which you desire, be it excitement, joy, confidence, compassion, freedom, power, expansion or connection. If you come against resistance from past trauma, don't judge yourself. Instead, observe and notice as soon as you witness the pain – you will immediately feel lighter. Fully accept those feelings and move into a space of unconditional love for yourself. Then, go back and activate the vibratory feelings that you desire.

This act of caring how you feel and choosing to align with what is wanted is the act of self-love. Doing things that make you feel happy and fulfilled, and having a healthy set of boundaries, is essential. This includes actively taking care of your body, nourishing your mind and spirit, and being completely authentic in all that you do. Taking the time to connect with yourself and listen to what you need, then getting those needs met, is essential for your wellbeing.

Loving yourself is a short cut to enlightenment. Every single brand of spiritual practise out there is aimed towards loving yourself. The best state you can align with is that of pure positive focus. We are here to become more of who we truly are. This requires awareness. All the great teachers of the world will tell you that everything you want is within you. When we try to satisfy our emotional needs externally, we will always be left wanting.

If we choose compassion and let go of the labels, we shift to a heart space reality, and a fifth dimensional state focused on being, rather than the 3D state of doing and having. Being is about absorbing into the present moment. It's an understanding that everything you experience in life is a reflection.

In truth, we have all incarnated hundreds of times as every different possibility of existence. We've been male, female, every race and culture. We've even existed as different species and existed in different dimensions. As we become more spiritually aware and less identified by our ego, our vibration rises, and the concept of difference and separation is no longer relevant. We live less from our head and more from our heart space.

When our ego takes centre stage, we become too worried about other people's opinions of us. We all go through life with an underlining sense of lack and insufficiency in some way. That said, we all have an innate drive to improve ourselves. We are all pre-conditioned to go through life looking for love and approval. Life is a balancing act of caring about ourselves and others.

When you feel empowered, you are full of your own personal truth. You are able to control the reality that you are currently living in. It is absolutely in your hands, whether you feel good or bad.

The biggest regret most people have when they are dying is not having had the courage to pursue their dreams. Life is over in the blink of an eye, so grab it with both hands and say yes to the opportunities that come your way. And remember, you never walk this path alone.

When you think about your identity and why you deserve to exist, you're not your thoughts. You can't be your feelings because otherwise, who is the you that feels them? You're not what you have, and you're not what you do. You're not even who you love or who loves you. There's something underneath all that.

Take the time now to connect in with yourself. Our heart is our connection to our higher selves. When we stop and listen to our heart, we align with our true desires for expansion.

Once you feel that you have reached a place of understanding with your heart, take some time to express gratitude for keeping you full of life.

On an emotional level feel either gratitude or love, then visualise this beautiful warm glowing energy flowing into your heart. Imagine that amazing energy being soaked up by the heart and then pumped through the rest of the body. Imagine that love diffuses through all of the capillaries, blood vessels, arteries and veins, and into every other organ. The heart is the one carrying the love there, throughout the totality of your being. Imagine that love soaking into each organ and every tiny little cell. At a cellular and metaphysical level, you are a being of pure, unconditional love.

The more connected you are with your heart, the more connected you are with your personal truth, and the more connected you are with your soul. Connecting with your heart is an essential part of your spiritual progression because it carries the burden of all the emotional trauma that you have experienced throughout your life. Releasing that trauma is the by-product of connecting with your heart, and taking care of its wants and needs. We are in a relationship with our heart. Our heart is our best friend. More than that, it is our life partner. We must treat our relationship with our heart like we would treat a relationship with a significant other. We need to nurture the relationship and strengthen the connection.

VIBRATIONAL LEVELS OF STATES OF EMOTION

Lower level feelings of fear and worry naturally dissipate when we start to live at a higher vibrational state. When we have a shift in consciousness, we relate to the world in a higher dimensional state. The Omega Scale of Consciousness is an interesting way to understand the different vibrational states of emotion.

Scale of Consciousness:

Enlightenment 700
Peace 600
Joy 540
Love 500
Reason 400
Acceptance 350
Willingness 300
Neutrality 250
Courage 200
Pride 175
Anger 150
Desire 125
Fear 100
Grief 75
Apathy 50
Guilt 30
Shame 20

Here, different emotional states are given a vibrational reading. The more expanded states, occurring above the state of neutrality, move us towards ultimate consciousness. Lower level feelings of fear and worry can disappear when you start to live at a higher vibrational state. When we have a shift in consciousness and raise our vibration, we relate to the world in a higher dimensional state. So, these vibrational states can also be understood in terms of dimensional reality.

THE STATE OF ALLOWING

Most of us have one area of our life that we excel in. But what about those areas in life we are not so good at? The secret is to let go of what is not working and focus on what is.

In reality, there are only two states: allowing or resistance. Often, when we enter a state of allowing, the resistance ends up going away. When we have a set idea of how things should be, we develop resistance when things don't work out the way we think they should. When we're in resistance, we're feeling negative emotion; we're letting our ego take control.

We keep going back to the ego, thinking things should be a certain way and feeling the subsequent negative emotion. The more we feel the negative emotion, the more we think we'll figure it out. But as Albert Einstein said, 'We can't solve our problems with the same thinking we used when we created them.' The key is not to bang the drum, thinking why does this keep happening, but to raise your vibration.

When people are focused on releasing the resistance, they're focused on the resistance. This is a Law of Attraction universe, and what you focus on brings you more of the same. When you focus instead on raising your vibration, connecting with a more substantial source part of you, you naturally start to let go of what isn't serving you and begin activating a higher vibration within.

The key is to shift the focus. If there's an area in your life that's lacking, focus on the part of your life where you're already high vibrational. In doing so, you'll find the old problems go away.

Archangel Raziel is here to inspire you to ditch the fear and love yourself on a deeper level. But, be warned, when you're ready to make self-empowering changes in your life, then resistance will rise like wildfire in equal proportion to your desire to thrive. Archangel Raziel is here to help you with this. Trust in the process of being uncomfortable with uncertainty, knowing that there is a safety net, even when you can't see it.

My favourite quote of all time is: 'If you knew who walked beside you, at all times, on this path that you have chosen, you could never experience fear and doubt again.' - *A Course In Miracles.*

The secret is to move from rigidity to softness. Think about what is more powerful – water or rock? We are 75% water, and so is the planet. Visualise yourself as water, and you can enter softly. The more grasp you have and the more you hold on, the less control you have. To experience water, be softer, more flexible, and in doing so, the more you will find you can accomplish. Be more open and willing to change your mind, or confessing, 'I don't know, I will have to look it up.' The secret to happiness is flowing, not forcing.

THE IMPORTANCE OF LIVING IN THE NOW

Most of the time, we are not fully present in existing in the here and now. We're too busy thinking of our to-do list in the future, or ruminating about what's gone on in the past. However, the present moment is all that really exists, and this is where the Angels can be found. They are with us right here, right now.

I believe that, as we are extensions of Source energy, our life purpose is to expand and grow. We are continually striving and wanting more. The secret to happiness is enjoying the process. There is no point thinking, 'I'll be happy when...' There will always be something else that we want to reach. Decide to be happy now. We came into this world to experience the joy of creating our desires and watching them transpire. There is just as much satisfaction to be had in anticipation of knowing that 'what you are is seeking you', as Rumi put it.

It's possible to find joy, no matter what your outward circumstances appear to be. As you hold joy in your heart, your negative circumstances will fade away, as you are no longer a vibrational match to them. This being a Law of Attraction universe, the Universe will match whatever vibration you put out. That's why, when you vibrate at a high frequency, everything seems to flow to you effortlessly, and you stumble on the perfect people and opportunities.

As we tap into Source energy, we raise our energetic vibration. We gain access to the infinite power of the Universe that is within us. In remembering our divinity, our heart fills with eternal joy and endless possibility. Each of us is a child of God, made perfect in our own unique and individual way.

Living with this awareness, we see that this is indeed an abundant universe. There becomes no need for lower-level energies such as greed, jealousy or hatred to affect us. We understand that separation is an illusion, and feeling the truth that we are all connected allows us to feel a deep sense of compassion, peace and lasting happiness.

A MEDITATION TO CONNECT TO OUR DIVINITY

Close your eyes and allow your inner awareness to begin. So, as you gently close your eyes, bring your attention to your breathing and feel a sense of stillness of being. Feel the natural ebb and flow of the breath, breathing in light and love, and releasing any negative or limited thinking. Inhale and exhale, and connect with your own rhythm of your own breath.

As you are breathing gently, start to consider that you are first and foremost a beautiful divine soul, a light. Every single person is Source energy. Source energy is within you. Source energy, which is one omnipresent nurturing energy.

You are Source, and when the human mind gets in the way, sometimes you don't remember who you are, your true Source, you are the one.

So, as you work with the rhythm of the breath, have the awareness that you are the light, you are the creativity. You are all that ever has been, all there will ever be.

Feel the joy, the happiness, who you are, and breathe that beautiful sense of power, light and enthusiasm throughout the body, being nurtured with joy, every organ, muscle, neuro fibres. Just feel the exuberance of who you are, this eternal light, this true soul. You are Source energy, and just be with that for a few moments. Bring yourself to that awareness now.

Take a deep breath, wiggle your fingers and toes, and come back into this space now.

DREAM INTERPRETATION

The Japanese have understood for a long time that when you sleep, your soul leaves your body to re-join the one universal Source energy. It is in actual fact not your body that needs rest, but your soul. It's extremely wearing on the soul to have to go through the restrictions and the hardships placed upon it while in this physical reality. So, when we dream, we are essentially experiencing an out of body reality where our consciousness is disassociated from our body, and our motor function is disabled.

Our dreams are a direct reflection of what is going on with us vibrationally. There is no resistance when we sleep, so dreams are an actual representation of what we have been thinking and feeling. In this way, dreams are a preview of pre-manifested reality, in so much that our minds choose a structure that is an exact reflection to the vibration we are currently holding. This is why dreams symbolically represent what we are currently experiencing. We are given metaphoric images of how we are feeling, which helps us process emotions.

When we are dreaming, we are interacting with our own thought-scapes. We are also able to interact with spirit and our guides as we are existing in the 5D consciousness. I find it incredibly comforting to be able to connect with my family and friends in spirit this way. There have also been many times that I have woken with amazing flashes of inspiration passed on from my guides.

Dreams are an incredible tool to assist us with our own expansion, as they can help us be honest about what we are unwilling to own up to. They show us what we are currently a match to in our day to day lives.

It's a great idea to keep a dream journal. Many people don't remember their dreams, but you'll be amazed how much you will remember if, the minute you wake up, you start writing them down. It's important to pay attention to the colours and how you feel in your dreams later on. Write down your dream as though you are currently experiencing it, rather than something that has happened in the past. Then you can explore becoming everything you experienced within that dream, with the perspective and feelings from that particular standpoint. Every aspect is part of you.

If you've had a nightmare, consciously go over that dream and change the circumstance so that it now feels good. If you've encountered something in your dream that scares you, use any way you can to alter that perspective to something that causes you to feel good instead. In this way you're providing yourself with resolution, which was the entire reason that the nightmare existed in the first place.

Dreams are a window to our conscious reality. If you have a question you would like help answering, spend five minutes thinking about that question and then set the intention that you will have a dream about that. Many inventions have been created this way. Every one of us dreams, whether we are aware of it or not.

'Dreams are also an opportunity for us to play out our desires and an unfinished dream is called life.' - Teal Swan

AFFIRMATIONS FOR ARCHANGEL RAZIEL

'Thank you, Archangel Raziel, for bringing past life knowledge through to help me with my life purpose.'

'Thank you, Archangel Raziel, for expanding my knowledge and appreciation for the Universe.'

'Thank you, Archangel Raziel, for helping me to be in touch with my feelings.'

'Thank you, Archangel Raziel, for helping me to understand and work with spiritual law to my best advantage.'

CHAPTER 17:
ARCHANGEL ARIEL

Environmentalism and Prosperity

Super Powers	Connect to nature / connection to fairies and other elementals / heal animals / healthy planet / stand your ground / assertiveness
Name Translation	Lioness of God
Crystal	Rose Quartz
Colour	Pale pink
Helping People	Conservation efforts and projects to cleanse and heal the earth. Helps people to get out of their comfort zone and find the courage 'to go for it'. Helping those with issues of diversity and inclusion.
Attributes	Connected to the fairies, elementals and nature magic, often pictured holding a cornucopia.

Archangel Ariel's name translates to 'the Lioness of God' and she helps us to feel stronger and more assertive. Her fiery presence is courageous and protective, just like a lion. She is strong, proud and fearless, strongly connected to the Earth, with a desire to do anything she can to help us feel safe. We can learn from her that being assertive does not mean steamrolling someone else with our opinion. We can understand that it is, however, essential to establish healthy boundaries. Boundaries are guidelines built on a mix of beliefs, opinions, social learning, past experiences and attitudes, that allow us to know what is acceptable for how others treat us.

Ariel is a powerful Archangel of manifestation, prosperity and abundance. This will make sense when you notice the complete abundance present within the natural world which Ariel is aligned. She is the protector of nature, including animals and the environment. Connecting to Ariel out in nature will help to refresh you completely, giving you a new excitement and positive perspective to manifest change and blessings in your life. Ariel has a pale pink aura and is linked to rose quartz. She is often pictured holding a cornucopia.

FINDING COURAGE

If there's something in our life that we need to stand up for, or an opinion we need to voice, or message we think we need to share, Archangel Ariel can help give us the courage to step into our truth and integrity. Archangel Ariel can help those that are wanting to protect the Earth. She also helps with issues of diversity and inclusion, bringing safety and strength, so that people can be acknowledged and accepted for their differences and the gifts that they bring. She can help people stand their ground and remain peaceful at the same time.

Feeling guilty when you say no, or saying yes when you mean no, acting against your integrity and values to please others, and not speaking up when you have something to say are indicators that you've violated your own boundaries. You are not staying true to what feels right to you. Boundaries are no different from our feelings. That's why it's essential to be in touch with your feelings and emotions. Healthy boundaries support your happiness and integrity, as well as your needs, desires and personal truth. It is only by honouring how you truly feel that you can live by your own truth, regardless if it is causing difficulty or not. A boundary is not about resisting what you do not want. A healthy boundary is in alignment with oneness, following your sense of happiness and truth, and hence bringing you in alignment with Source energy. This healthy sense of self serves you and the Universe.

If we want to live a happy life, we need to admit how we feel and what we desire, and align with that.

SAVING THE PLANET AND OURSELVES

One of the best things we can do to help the planet is to stop eating meat. The strain that this food production is having on the planet cannot be sustained. Biologically, we are not meant to be meat-eaters. Our saliva is, in fact, similar to that of a cow as it is alkaline, as opposed to the acidic saliva found in carnivores. We also have the same teeth structure and long intestines to that of a cow. Meat-eating animals have sharp teeth used for tearing out the flesh, and their intestines are shorter, which is essential to digest fresh meat quickly. Also, eating sugar, carbohydrates and wheat eventually become mucus in the system, building up a wall that is not needed. If you want to have more energy, feel dynamic, clearer, look younger and have a sexier body, change your diet accordingly.

Animals have a soul purpose just like us. When we eat an animal, we absorb the fear energy that it has suffered. If we commit to living life to our fullest potential, this means keeping our energetic vibration as high as we can. It is not part of the contract to eat animals.

The natural state of animals is that of alignment, being in the space of allowing and love. They gravitate towards what they enjoy rather than what they don't. Animals are much more in a state of allowing than humans. They do not hold a state of resistance to things like disease and death, living more by their instincts. Animals are amplifiers of our emotional state, reflecting to us the state of our own emotions. In the space of allowing and love, this is a magnetic calling for us to line up with that perspective and state. Animals are so good at self-gratification that it is only natural for them to extend that love toward us.

MEDITATION WITH ARCHANGEL ARIEL FOR ABUNDANCE

First of all, connect to the abundance frequency with Archangel Ariel and imagine her beautiful warm light pink light surrounding your entire body. This warm pink light is full of healing, love and energy. Take a deep breath in and exhale. Affirm to yourself, 'I connect now to the abundance frequency that is always available to me.' As you feel this warm pink energy surrounding your body, take your energy up 300ft where you see, sense or feel the light. This is connecting to Source energy. You may see the light, or feel the light. Connect to this amazing bright light, and allow it to start coming up through your crown at the top of your head. Ask this light, this abundance frequency, to clear away all thoughts of lack and limit.

From anywhere you see problems or debt, allow this light to come into your eye and cleanse that away, restoring you to full potential.

From anywhere you block the guided answers and truth from helping you, allow this light to come into your ears and cleanse that away, restoring you to full potential.

From anywhere you block the energy of speaking confidently about your new future, allow the light to come into your voice and your throat, cleansing that away and restoring you to full potential.

From everywhere you've lost compassion or commitment to change, allow the light to come into your heart, cleansing that away and restoring you to full potential.

From anywhere you block your life from flowing from love versus fear, allow the light to come into your solar plexus in your belly and chest area, cleansing and restoring you to full potential.

From anywhere you block your light and feel powerless over circumstances, where you gave in or gave up trying, allow the light to come into your stomach area, cleansing and restoring you to full potential.

From anywhere you lack the 'go for it' attitude, allow the light to come into your hips, cleansing and restoring you to full potential.

Feel this light coming in through your feet now, grounding you with a fresh, new energy that's inspiring and hopeful, full of abundance.

Now, let this light go from you, deep into the centre of the planet, and imagine that there is a light that feels as comforting as a mother's love at the Earth's core. It feels safe. It feels secure. It feels grounded. It feels happy. Take a deep breath as you connect to it.

Now, allow this light to travel up through the earth, through your feet, through your legs, your hips, your stomach and your heart, your throat and your head. You are now connected to the light above and below so that you are covered with light.

Imagine that this ball of light is expanding out around you, 10ft around you, 20ft around you, 30ft around you, 60ft around you, until you find a cosy place where it just feels comfortable. You are now connected to the abundance frequency. You are now connected to Source energy. You are now connected to unlimited possibilities.

Visualise a light coming in now that will dissolve all your blocks in your beliefs about money. Allow the light in. When you think of blocking your abundance or limiting yourself, you may feel a heavy sensation in a specific part of your body. Does a part of your body feel heavy? If so, that's where the belief is locked in and is stuck in your reality. Take a deep breath and allow the light to flood into this area. Say in your mind the following:-

'Everywhere that the belief is that I can only make a limited amount of money, creating a set point for limiting my abundance, I now clear this across all time and space, dimension and reality.'

Now, fill in with the positive: 'What would it take for me to receive an unlimited amount of abundance? What would it take for me to be able to receive a dream amount of money?' By saying, 'What would it take for me to receive...' you're letting the Universe figure that out for you.

If you've ever decided that you don't have enough and it's not possible to get what you want, ask yourself if you picked this up from your parents, yourself, or someone else? When you think of the belief that you're not able to create more than enough money, where does it feel heavy in your body? Put your focus on this light instantly transmuting this belief or block, and clear this across all time and space, dimension and reality.

Now, fill in with the positive: 'What would it take for me to have more than enough money? What would it take for the Universe to supply me with everything that I need? What would it take for me to always have extra?'

Now, turn your attention to your career. Has there been a point where you lost hope that there is nothing better out there for you? Are you stuck in a job that you don't like because you think that there is nothing better for you? When did you decide that you can't get what you want? Did you pick that up from your parents, yourself, or someone else? Now, clear that across all time and space, dimension and reality.

'What would it take for me to make a living by being me? What would it take for me to actually get what I want from my career? What would it take to get money for being me? What would it take to be paid more than I need for being me?'

At what age did you decide that money was hard to come by? Perhaps you were told that money doesn't grow on trees, or that you had to work hard for it? Did you pick that up from your parents, yourself, or someone else? Now, please clear and transmute that across all time and space, dimension and reality.

'What would it take for me to know that money is easy to come by? What would it take for me to know that abundance is a natural state? What would it take for me to know that abundance is my birth right?'

Quite often, we learn how to react about something from our parents or caregivers. Have you've ever felt worried about money? Did you learn that reaction from your parents, yourself, or someone else? Where did you learn to stress out about money? At what age did this pattern take hold? Do you sense or feel it heavily in your body? Now, bring the light into that area and clear and transmute that across all time and space, dimension and reality. Everywhere you learned to worry about money, clear and transmute that across all time and space, dimensions and reality.

When in your life did you decide that it was not good or kind to love money? When did you become fearful about generating wealth? Did you pick that up from your dad, your mum, yourself, or someone else? Take your energy around the body and clear and transmute that across all time and space, dimensions and reality.

'What would it take for me to know that it's completely OK for me to love money? What would it take for me to know that it's completely OK for me to love abundance? What would it take for me to know that it's completely OK for me to generate wealth? Money is just an energy, and it allows me the freedom in life to make a difference in this world and live the life I want to live. It's OK for me to be rich. It's OK for me to be wealthy.'

What kind of energy did the people who brought you up have around money? Did you duplicate that energy? Wherever it feels heavy or tight in your body, take your energy and the light into that spot. Now, take your energy around the body and clear and transmute that across all time and space, dimension and reality.

'What would it take for you to be your own positive beliefs about money? What would it take for you to have an abundant mindset? What would it take for you to live your own reality about money?'

Do you have a block that sabotages you from not going for what you want? What is this block? Where did you pick it up? Now, clear and transmute that across all time and space, dimensions and reality.

'What would it take for me to get whatever I want in life? What would it take for me to accept whatever career path, whatever opportunity that would be the best, most incredible life for me? What would it take for abundance to be my birth right?'

Know that by asking these questions you are inviting the Universe to provide you with an answer. Take a deep breath in now, feeling lighter, brighter, and ready to take on the world! Smile and come back into this space.

AFFIRMATIONS FOR ARCHANGEL ARIEL

'Thank you, Archangel Ariel, for helping me to reclaim my power and stand my ground.'

'Thank you, Archangel Ariel, for helping the animals know that they are loved, safe and well.'

'Thank you, Archangel Ariel, for guiding me to connect to the healing power and spirit of nature, and helping the Earth's environment.'

'Thank you, Archangel Ariel, for helping my family to have all our needs met.'

CHAPTER 18:
ARCHANGEL METATRON

For sensitive children, energy clearing and releasing limited beliefs

Super Powers   Re-align energy / purifies lower energy / balance chakras / malleability of the physical universe / bending time / overseer of sensitive children / sacred geometry.

Name Meaning   The Throne Next to the Divine

Crystal   Watermelon Tourmaline

Colour   Seafoam green and violet

Helping People   Indigo and crystal children and those who have incarnated to awaken our planet.

Attributes   Metatron and Sandalphon were once humans who ascended into the Angelic realm by virtue of their faith in God and their perfectly pious conduct. Metatron had been the Hebrew prophet Enoch and became an ascended

255

master whom God transformed into the powerful Angel Metatron. He works with the sacred geometry of the Merkabah and is associated with the Soul Star.

Archangel Metatron is believed to have once walked the Earth as a human, the prophet Enoch. The vast knowledge he attained of the Divine ascended him to becoming an Archangel. 'Meta thronon' is Hebrew for 'the throne next to the Divine'. He is believed to be the spiritual brother of Archangel Sandalphon, who also walked the Earth as a human.

If ever you are running late for something, ask Archangel Metatron to help you get there with time to spare. He has the ability to bend time for you so that you can arrive somewhere on time or get a project finished. He is also known as the protector of children and very sensitive people.

He balances the energy of our planet with the help of sacred geometry called the Merkabah. This is a hexagon shape with two overlaying triangles and circles at all the points. This special geometrical shape is constantly spinning very fast to harmonise, clear and balance our energy. It represents pure divine energy, and moves in all four directions at all times supporting you where you want to go. He also creates energy grids to support energy. He is associated with the colours white with pink or violet and green, and the crystal Watermelon Tourmaline.

INDIGO'S, CRYSTAL CHILDREN AND EARTH ANGELS

As an Indigo, I grew up very sensitive to the energy around me. Now, as an adult, I have flashes to a past life. I know very clearly that I have been here before, many times. I have always felt creativity flowing through me like a river. Indigos can see things clearly from a bigger picture perspective. We are tapped into our abilities - our Source energy - and are highly inventive as a result. Honesty has always been something that I highly value. No matter how hard it may be to take at times, it is always better than knowing that someone has not been genuine. Indigos are more sensitive, more intuitive, and more eager to discover their spiritual gifts. This is not about learning; it's more about remembering.

Indigo's can go on to have crystal children. These are highly sensitive. They can see lights around people, hear voices, have imaginary friends, see orbs. They are also very sensitive to their environment. They react to any toxic foods and drinks and toxic energy altogether. In the current state of the world, many have food allergies or skin conditions.

Crystal children rely on their intuition so much that, to thrive, they can't be conditioned through medication. They are very empathic and radiate love and compassion. They can heal others just by being in their presence. If they don't feel comfortable in their own body, then they need to move physically, thriving on kinaesthetic interactive learning. They are very creative and inventive. Often, they have a natural ability to paint, or are talented singers or dancers. As time goes on, the human consciousness will continue to evolve, and one day we will communicate telepathically with each other.

Such sensitive people can feel a lot of pain through anxiety or feelings of not belonging. When you're feeling out of alignment, ask Archangel Metatron for help. Remember that you're here to be of service. You came here to create. If you don't fit into a specific area, move to somewhere where you will feel inspired. You are the mind of the new thinkers, where advancement in society becomes possible. All you have to do is follow your joy and your bliss. As long as you are in a creative state of mind, your life is on purpose, and you feel as though you are needed and that your life has meaning. It doesn't matter how old you are – it is essential to explore this creative flow and be an instrument for good.

Earth Angels are more connected to the Angelic realm. They are very sensitive to energies and can see through people, picking up on their emotions very quickly. They love to observe people's behaviours and notice small details. They are interested and curious about the world around them. They have a natural tendency to fall in love quickly and could be crazy in love with you, but they will not say. Earth Angels need to have their space as they need to have time to assimilate and balance their emotions. They are also incapable of lying and will disconnect from anyone that does not tell them the truth. It may take them some time to embrace their uniqueness and step into their power, and they do not wish to stand out.

AUTISM

Those classed as being Autistic are also much more sensitive. We look at disorders as though something has gone wrong, but that is not the perspective that our true, eternal self holds. Anybody with a 'disorder' is being served immensely from the experience because we only ever create something in our reality if it serves us in some way. For thousands of years, humans have been left-brain orientated, and so less connected to their eternal aspects and more focused on the physical dimension. It is, however, right-brain thinking that helps with our awareness of our connection with Source energy.

Some have chosen not to activate the portion of our DNA that allows us to phase completely with the physical dimension. Autistic people are not entirely phased with the physical dimension, so they have one foot in and one foot out of physical reality. This means they have much more energy flowing through their body, which creates an increase in neural activity, causing their systems to be overstimulated. This impaired neurological function may lead to seizures, or difficulty in performing tasks, nervous gestures and ticks. The nervous system is the translator between non-physical and physical, between pure consciousness and the expression of that consciousness into the physical dimension. When it's impaired, that translation cannot take place clearly, and the connection with the physical dimension is impaired. For autistic people, it's not their consciousness that's impaired; it's their translation of their consciousness into physical expressions, such as language, that is impaired. It's caused by improper phasing with the physical dimension.

It is estimated that one in 68 people are autistic, and this is a conservative estimate. Autism is a spectrum and doesn't affect everyone the same way. It's characterised by three main things: challenges with social interaction, difficulty with verbal and non-verbal communication, and repetitive and routine behaviour. As it is a spectrum, not everyone is severely affected by it. The root of the challenges lies in the sensory input; autism is a different way of perceiving the reality around us. The challenges are a result of how individuals with autism see, hear, smell, touch and feel the world in a way that is different from the mainstream. Imagine a world where the light is too bright, where the colours are too agitating, and every pattern too distracting. Then, imagine if you weren't able to ignore the background sound of the air-conditioning humming, or the fluorescent lights buzzing, or the noise of people walking around you. Imagine no one understanding why you behave the way you do as a result of the different way that you sense and process the world.

Working with what they know and what they focus on, which is typically their obsessive routine, can be done through spacial sequencing, working on predictability and organised space. This is known as affinity therapy, based on finding something that the person is passionate about, or something that is repeatable and predictable that will be a source of pleasure and fascination, to gain significant emotional understanding. This could be watching Disney movies, where there are the same concepts of good and evil, or working with the predictable, logical world of Lego. By joining in with whatever the person loves to do every day, it's possible to make a connection.

In life, we have expectations about normal behaviour, and we assume that something has gone wrong when someone doesn't conform to our ideals. Autistic people did not come here to fit into a box; they came to get everyone else out of their own box. We are moving into a new reality where we are phasing into our non-physical aspects, being a physically manifested spiritual species. Autistic people are a species link between what we are now and what we are becoming.

They require that we accept who they are with all their unique expressions, requiring us to overcome our resistance to change. In the process of that accommodation, we have to question everything about ourselves and allow our society to change. Our current school system orientates towards conformity and standardisation, not individuals. But if the majority of people can't conform to that, that model must change. This is a strategy of non-physical energy: to increase the numbers of people on the autism spectrum and those with ADD and ADHD to help change our society into one that accommodates the individual and stops going in the direction of conformity.

We have to recognise that there is nothing wrong with people that are autistic or have ADD and ADHD, and we should stop expecting them to behave in a certain way. From their perspective, they will only focus on what they want to focus on. In this time-space reality, that is a by-product of our thoughts – we are meant to come in and focus on what we want to focus, and let that focus create and design the physical reality. When we cause people to conform to focus on what we want them to focus on, we are getting in the way of their creation. By trying to get a child to focus on something other than what fascinates them in the first place, we are doing them a huge disservice. We must allow them to initiate their learning, and trust them to know what is right for them. We must prioritise in our hearts what we know will bring them the most joy, more so than what the rest of society says you must do. Letting go of our rigid demands for conformity requires great bravery. Once this has been mastered, we will be infinitely in touch with our true selves, with our non-physical selves, with our spiritual selves. The vision is to live in a cohesive society with everyone following their own bliss.

Every autistic person has a gift to share with this world, so choose to see the gifts that they have and their capability. They are the forerunners of the new level of brain function within the human species. Self-expression is the opposite of conformity, and by allowing and embracing this, suffering will end.

RELEASING RESISTANCE GUIDED MEDITATION WITH ARCHANGEL METATRON

You're about to embark on a beautiful journey; a journey of releasing resistance. Sit with your back straight and make sure you are comfortable. Close your eyes and begin to breathe deeply. Inhale through your nose, and exhale out through your mouth. Breathe again, in through your nose, and out through your mouth. One more time, in and out. Allow your breathing to fall into a natural and relaxed rhythm. No effort is required. Your body and mind are becoming relaxed, sinking into the comfortable experience you are creating. Nothing else matters now, and there is nothing you have to do.

We are now going to connect with the beautiful energy of Archangel Metatron. He will help us release limiting beliefs and remove any blockages, so that we can tune into Divine magic and manifestation. Metatron views reality with a full understanding of God and the Universe. He can help clear your energy, assisting you in releasing everything that no longer serves you.

Picture the watermelon colours of pink and green shining down upon you. The light is warm and familiar. It is comforting, loving and peaceful. Imagine this light beginning to wash over you now, starting at the top of your head. It shines on your face and neck, relaxing the muscles in your forehead and jaw. Now, it moves down into your shoulders and down into your chest and back. It radiates warmth down your arms and hands and fingers, relaxing your upper body. Down your stomach and your pelvis. Feel any tension wash away. Down through your hips and thighs, your body sinking deeper into your relaxation. Down your legs and feet, and through the tips of your toes. You are completely at ease, and now you are ready for a beautiful journey.

All that you want in this life is yours if you release your negative beliefs. Whether you want a state of health, financial abundance, or a relationship, releasing negative beliefs will allow them to flow easily into your experience. There is no effort you need to apply to achieve them. All you need to do is relax into this creative moment.

See yourself now walking along a path to the banks of a beautiful river. At the edge of the water, you see a small boat. This vessel will accompany you on your journey. Place your boat into the water and step in. With a gentle push, your boat begins to float away from the banks and downstream.

You look around and notice that the water is moving at a slow and comfortable pace. The water is clean, and the banks alongside are green, lush and filled with life. The air that surrounds you is warm and inviting. You feel appreciation for where you are in your journey, and you feel a sense of adventure for all you will experience.

Off in the horizon, you notice a familiar golden light. You feel a calling to let go now and allow the river to move you downstream. You recognise that all of your desires are downstream towards this light. You feel ease wash over you. There is nothing you have to do; all you need to do is let go.

Now, I want you to imagine that you see an obstacle in the river. This obstacle represents poor health. You begin to sense that, as you focus your attention on the obstacle, your boat moves towards it. Begin to shift your attention away from the obstacle, and imagine the state of health that you desire. The truth is that health and wellbeing flow naturally to you at all times. They are your birth right. Imagine yourself choosing fresh and nutritious foods, imagine yourself moving your body every day. Imagine your body as strong, flexible and agile. You move about the world comfortably and perform your daily activities with ease. It feels so good to allow wellbeing to flow to you.

You begin to notice that, as you place your attention away from the obstacle, your boat begins to change direction and move around it. You have now travelled past it, feeling alive and well. The river is moving faster. You are moving further downstream towards all that you desire. You are filled with a deep sense of joy and wellbeing.

Now, I want you to imagine a second obstacle approaching you in the river. This obstacle represents financial hardship. Shift your attention away from the obstacle. You know intuitively that financial abundance is all around you. Financially, you recognise that there is no limit to what you can achieve if you believe it. You become keenly aware that there are many paths for which abundant resources can flow to you, and you feel that money and success will come easily if you allow it.

As you focus on these thoughts, your boat begins to move around the obstacle. The river is flowing fast now. You are feeling free and powerful, and you are moving closer to what you desire downstream. Notice the feeling of adventure and appreciation along this journey.

Now, imagine that you see the third obstacle along your path. This obstacle represents troubled relationships you may have had. Shift your attention away from the obstacle. The truth is, when you allow yourself to be who you really are, you will attract others who will resonate with you. When you realise that you are the source of your happiness, you will no longer feel dependant on another in this way. I want you to imagine yourself in a relationship that you desire. This relationship can be a family member, a friend or a lover. Imagine how you want to feel in this relationship. Imagine feeling happy, fulfilled, safe and secure.

As you focus this way, your boat begins to change direction again, moving past the obstacle in front of you. The river is now moving very fast and free. You are moving swiftly downstream towards all that you desire. The health, financial conditions, relationships, and all the other things that you desire are closer to you now than ever before. You feel worthy and eager about where you are going.

Thank Archangel Metatron for helping you to clear your mental, spiritual and energy bodies of any fear or blockages, so that you can fully step into your authentic truth. Archangel Metatron has helped you experience life from a perspective that is beyond illusion, and that is in alignment with your genuine deep, profound connection with the Divine and all of life. Stay in this moment, and bask in how much you have accomplished, feeling anticipation for what is yet to come.

When you are ready, take a deep breath and bring your attention back into this room. Wiggle your fingers and toes, take an energising big stretch. When you are ready, open your eyes.

AFFIRMATIONS FOR ARCHANGEL METATRON

'Thank you, Archangel Metatron, for adjusting the time so that I arrive on schedule.'

'Thank you, Archangel Metatron, for helping me to cope with feelings of not fitting in, and guiding me to connect with my own group of like-minded beings.'

'Thank you, Archangel Metatron, for helping to comfort and reassure my sensitive child.'

'Thank you, Archangel Metatron, for balancing my Chakras, and helping me to feel harmonious and revitalised.'

CHAPTER 19:
ARCHANGEL SANDALPHON

Music and delivered prayers

Super Powers   Answered prayers / Music / Reawakened spiritual gifts / appreciating victory and miracles

Name Translation   Co-brother

Crystal   Turquoise, Smokey Quartz, Petrified Wood, Tourmalinated Quartz

Colour   Turquoise, copper gold and the colours of nature

Helping People   People going through trials in their own life, delivering prayers to God. Helps get your message across with grace and beauty. Musicians looking for inspiration.

Attributes   Co-brother to Archangel Metatron. The tallest of Angels, reaching from Earth to Heaven, associated with the Earth Star. Said to have incarnated on Earth as the prophet Elijah and to have been turned into an Archangel by God.

When you're going through a difficult time and you feel as though your prayers haven't been heard or answered, ask Archangel Sandalphon to help, as he is known to carry prayers to God. Be open to the fact that the answer may come in a different form than you may expect. As Sandalphon is known as the Angel of music, it may even be that his messages come to you in the form of music or poetry.

Sandalphon is said to have been a mortal man, the prophet Elijah, who lived such a spiritual life that he ascended as an Archangel, along with Metatron. Sandalphon's name means 'co-brother', which refers to Sandalphon's status as the spiritual brother of the Archangel Metatron. He can help us to appreciate how miraculous life is and celebrate every victory and little miracle.

Archangel Sandalphon is associated with the colours in nature, including bronze and copper and the magnificent clear blue sky. Wearing turquoise or smoky quartz can help you connect to his energy. If you're feeling under pressure, he can help you feel strong, as he is linked to the Earth Star, bringing energy up through your feet to ground you. Archangel Sandalphon and Archangel Metatron work in synergy together, with Sandalphon connecting to the Earth Star Chakra, and Metatron connecting to the Soul Star chakra. They bridge the gap between Heaven and Earth. Sandalphon is said to be the tallest of Angels, reaching from Earth to Heaven.

GETTING YOUR PRAYERS ANSWERED

If you feel concerned that your prayers have not been heard, stop to consider whether everything is in alignment for them to materialise. It could be that limiting beliefs are undermining your conscious efforts. For example, if you're trying to conceive but subconsciously are worried about becoming a parent because of a traumatic childhood, then you don't feel that it's safe to bring a child into the world. It could even be that, in a previous life, you suffered greatly during childbirth, and on a deep level don't feel safe to be put in that situation again. There are some fantastic past life regression healers now, as well as spiritual councillors, who can guide you to nurture your inner child. Once things are brought to the light, they can then be released, leaving you free to progress unhindered in your pursuit of happiness.

Perhaps you've created a visual dream board of all the things you desire, and you have repeated affirmations about wealth, but you still maintain a poverty consciousness? This sends mixed signals to the Universe. The Universe responds to your feelings, not to your words. You may even be praying for someone else to recover from an illness but perhaps, on a soul level, this provides lessons that individual signed up to experience. There may be many factors that influence the outcome.

Examining our beliefs is essential to our success and wellbeing. All too often, we can pick up belief systems from our parents without even questioning the validity of them. Could it be that you have been taught to believe that 'money is the root of all evil' or 'money doesn't grow on trees', for example? These false limiting beliefs could be stopping you from receiving the abundance that you deserve. Affirmations are an excellent way to retrain the mind to focus on what is wanted, rather than what is not. These positive statements said in the present tense hold great power to manifest what is desired.

The Universe operates on a Law of Attraction basis. What you think about, both good and bad, will come into your reality – it's all a question of focus. Release your fears to the Angels and hold a vision of what you want, rather than where you are at the moment. Charge this with the emotion that you will feel once your desire is met, and you will shift your vibration to bring it forth into your life. It's not things that we want; instead, it's the emotional experience that we think it will provide. Ironically, when we choose to go straight for the feeling, what we were wanting will manifest anyway.

Living a life full of integrity requires being open about who you are without restriction. Remember what life was like as a child. There were no thoughts about suppressing yourself, and you had no secrets from the world. You did not exclude people from your heart, and you were honest because that was the most natural way to be. As children, we follow our emotional guidance system until we are taught not to do so. Constriction is painful, and it is, therefore, unnatural.

There are many ways we go on to constrict and isolate ourselves. When we do not express our emotions and try and conform to a life expected of us, we suffer physically as well as emotionally. When we fear exposure and choose to hide our true self, then we are not the full unique expression of ourselves that we came here to be.

The Universe is all-inclusive, and we are everything and everyone. When we live in a state of constriction, we are resistant to the very things that we are afraid of, and so they can hurt us. However, by living in a state of complete openness where we share, are honest, and are in a state of flow, nothing can be used against us. Far better to commit to the path of openness and live a healthy life of alignment.

Make a point of celebrating your life and show it off to others as a creative expression of yourself. Don't be afraid of your magnificence, your power and your wisdom. When you succeed, you inspire others. When you change your life so that you are more aligned with your interest, you inspire others. Ask Archangel Sandalphon to clear away any fears that are blocking you from thoroughly enjoying and living your spiritual gifts and qualities.

When you are living in a state of perfect alignment with your own conscious, you are whole and undivided. Displaying a lack of integrity is a form of self-betrayal. Honour all the different aspects of yourself, accept and integrate all your shadows as well as your light. Get completely honest about yourself. Follow through on your word, and don't make a promise or a commitment unless you can honour it.

THE POWER OF PRAYER

Archangel Sandalphon delivers prayers safely. Prayers are the setting forth of intention with pure focus, and then settling into the vibration of pure faith to receive.

The very fabric of reality can be shifted by pure positive focus and faith. This is when we say miracles have occurred. Thoughts are so much more powerful than physical laws. If you can focus with such purity of thought and allow the creative force to flow through you, you can bend all the physical laws you see before you.

When you are praying, who is it you are praying to? The answer should be to yourself, as you're praying to your Source self, the larger part of you, which is the same as God. If you believe God is something outside of yourself then prayer puts you in a state of submission, as you're giving the power away to something else. There is then a possibility that you might or might not be given what you have asked for. But what you are asking for is not about you deserving it or not. When we make this power divisible from us, we lose that creative power.

When real prayer is appropriately done, you acknowledge the fact that you are the creator. You are affecting your reality by focusing on the God force within you. When appropriately used, prayer is amazing. The problem with prayer is never with asking. The problem is with focus.

When prayers are not answered, it's never that the Universe is withholding things from you. The law of this Universe is, 'Ask, and It Is Given.' This does not depend on you being deserving or not. However, the Law of Attraction, which is the most powerful law in the Universe, states that only that which is a vibrational match can share the same space. That means, only things that are a vibrational match to where you stand can enter your reality.

When people believe that their prayers weren't answered, it's

272

because of the way that they were focusing when they asked for that prayer to be received. Beliefs must match outcomes. You may be praying for love, but if your constant focus is on how unworthy you are, then you are holding yourself in a vibrational tug of war. Everything you want exists, but unless you align yourself, you can't receive what you have asked for.

Many people think they're praying for what they want. In reality, they are focused on what they don't want. These people are simply using their words to ask the Universe, but the Universe responds to thought, not words, so it can't recognise 'doesn't' or 'not'. When you plead, 'Don't die,' it hears 'die'. That's why it's important to phrase things in a way that is positive. Realise that you are a perfect vibrational match to where you place your attention.

When you offer a prayer, keep holding the vision of perfection. If you are praying for someone to be healed, hold the vision of them being in perfect health. If you are praying for financial assistance, visualise the money already paid into your bank account and imagine how it would feel. If you're praying for a relationship, put yourself in a state where you have already received that. Hold that pure positive focus. Keep prayers simple, sincere and from the heart. This is when miracles occur. The way to ensure that your prayer will give you results is to believe that it will. We have to shift our beliefs to believing before we see. The 3D dimension is designed so that we broadcast thought. Thought becomes a thing, the by-product we look at which we call proof. This is why no one can ever agree because everyone's reality is subjective.

So, if you want to manifest anything, you have to begin thinking thoughts that what you want is true. We must shift our thoughts into a way to look for what we believe to be true before we see it. If we are solely focused on 'what is' and the proof of 'what is', we will get more of 'what is'. To shift your reality and have your prayers answered, you need to talk your way into believing before you see, and that will be your key to seeing.

Get yourself in a calm and centred space. Imagine then that you have a golden aura. This raises your vibration and aligns you better with the Angels. Ask your prayer in a way that gives thanks, then detach from the result. Hold your faith and prepare for it to be granted. For a prayer to work, you have to have total trust in the outcome. This means continuously listening to your guidance and intuition, and understanding that the solution cannot be granted outside of you. As a spark of God, all the power is inside of you. Do not wish for an external source to permit you.

Everything you need is already in the Universe; it is just a question of you aligning to receive it. Having total faith is not the same as blind faith, which is merely hope. Here you instinctively know that things might not work out as you hope. If you have total trust, then success is assured.

GRATITUDE

The quickest way to raise your vibration and lift yourself up out of fear is to stop and choose to think about something that you are truly grateful for. It's physically impossible to be in a state of fear and uncertainty and feel grateful at the same time. Even in the darkest moments, we can always find something we can feel grateful for. It may be an experience you had in your life, or the clean air that you have to breathe, or the pet that shows you unconditional love. Whatever it is, just feel your heart expand with joy and appreciation. Breathe deeply, and let that wonderful energy permeate every cell of your body. Trust that, by realigning yourself, everything else will fall into place.

'If the only prayer you said in your whole life was, 'thank you,' that would suffice.' - Meister Eckhart

When I'm driving I love to notice the reciprocal nature of kindness. When I am considerate and let out a driver who I can see has been waiting, I notice in no time at all that they do the same thing for another driver further along. Their gratitude and appreciation has been shared and this domino effect keeps going, all the while making the world a less stressful, more uplifting place to be.

There is a saying that good things happen to good people, and while every single person on the planet gets tested as some point, it is true that the world is our mirror. If we are in a state of fear and uncertainty, we will attract situations that challenge us. The more we can take control of our thoughts and emotions by deliberately selecting what we wish to experience, the more enjoyable life will become.

It's incredibly important to give thanks to the Universe when something does go right for you, as this is an indication to the Universe that you would like more of the same. It's great to do a little happy dance to mark your successes. It might sound silly, but acknowledge that this is your moment. Appreciate the alignment with your dreams, wishes and physical reality if you want to ensure continued success.

A magical thing to do is to start a gratitude journal. This is lovely to have beside your bed, so that every night before you go to sleep, you can write down ten things that you are grateful for that day. I've done this exercise when I was struggling to cope emotionally in my life, and it totally transformed my reality. It's easy to take things for granted, even the simplest things such as having clean water to drink. When we take a few moments to stop and consider all our blessings, the world begins to regain its sparkle again.

I make a point of thanking the Angels every day for their love and assistance, and ask that there be no limits for their help across all time, space and dimensions. This just keeps the wonderful energy flowing. Knowing I have their unending support in every moment makes the world an exciting place full of possibility. What more could anyone ask for?

MUSIC

Music is a celebration of life. It has an incredibly powerful effect on our wellbeing. Learning to play an instrument is the only thing we can do that actually links both sides of the brain to work at the same time. Listening to music alters our brainwave state and mood. The next time you feel in a bad mood, put on your favourite music and see how long that bad mood lasts!

Researchers found that listening to favourite songs altered the connectivity between auditory brain areas and a region responsible for memory and social emotion consolidation. Just like with smell, listening to a specific piece of music can instantly transport us back to a time and space in our lives where we previously enjoyed it. Listening to music can create peak emotions, which increase the amount of dopamine (the happy hormone) while also reducing blood pressure.

There is a specific frequency - 963Hertz, known as Solfeggio frequency - that is associated with awakening intuition and activating the pineal gland. It is said to awaken our crown chakra (Sahasrara) and raise the positive energy and vibrations to help us connect to our very source. It's important to remember that we are made of vibration and energy. The lowest frequency on the Sofeggio scale is 174Hertz which acts like an energetic anaesthesia. Thanks to its slow, soothing qualities, this frequency is wonderful for reducing pain in your physical body, and helping you to feel secure. Sound healing is becoming increasingly popular. Singing bowls and gong baths can aid in deep relaxation, transporting us away to another world.

AFFIRMATIONS FOR ARCHANGEL SANDALPHON

'Thank you, Archangel Sandalphon, for boosting my musical abilities.'

'Thank you, Archangel Sandalphon, for helping me to feel that my life is miraculous by appreciating every victory and little miracle.'

'Thank you, Archangel Sandalphon, for assisting me to see, hear or know what the answers to my prayers are.'

'Thank you, Archangel Sandalphon, for helping me live a life full of integrity with all my spiritual gifts fully awakened.'

PART 3:
GUARDIAN ANGELS

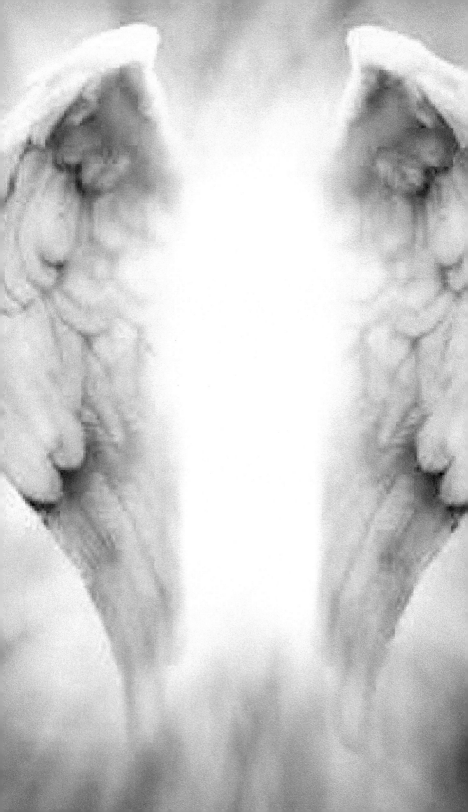

CHAPTER 20:
GUARDIAN ANGELS

In addition to working with these Archangels, you are encouraged to build a strong relationship with your own Guardian Angels.

A good way to do this is to get a journal and practise automatic writing every day. Set the intention to connect to your Guardian Angels and ask for their guidance and support. Relax, and ask for their help to quieten the mind. Welcome them, introduce yourself, then ask what they would like you to know. Then, allow your pen to write. Some people try writing with the other hand to assist in this process.

You can then begin to 'download' their perspective subconsciously using claircognizance and transcribe it as it comes in. It should feel effortless, like being 'in the flow'. As time goes by, you'll notice the words that don't sound like you.

If something negative comes up, know that it's coming from your ego. Ask Archangel Michael to cut your ego out of this and start again. Remember, the Angels are always trying to guide us towards joy.

Lorna Byrne states that we are already in contact with our Guardian

Angels – we are just letting human doubt get in the way. This little niggling voice inside our head that lets us know what we should do is the one that we need to respond to with action. Lorna tells us that we are given signs one hundred times a day from our Guardian Angels that let us know that we are going in the right direction. The problem is that we have free will and we don't always listen and take action. We can empower our Guardian Angels by giving them more permission. They have to respect our free will, so they can only help you if you ask or permit them to. It doesn't matter how you ask, so long as you do.

Your Guardian Angels look past all human errors and see within you your potential, your goodness, your love and light. They love you unconditionally and they are always by your side.

Your Guardian Angels are celestial non-human beings who are with you throughout your entire life, lifetime after lifetime. We each have at least two Guardian Angels.

One is a magnetic, quiet, and comforting Angel who helps us in times of great need when we need emotional support, such as when we face disappointment or grief. The other is a dynamic Guardian Angel who tends to be more of a coach, or a motivator, and is easier to hear.

You can hear your guides in your heart, mind and feelings, urging you to do the right thing, to take good care of yourself, and to live a life that is true to your beliefs. Our Angels are constantly whispering guidance to us; we are never alone. Their soul purpose is to help you experience peace, joy, health and happiness.

There have been many books written through automatic writing. These include:

Conversations with God by Neale Donald Walsh

Ten Messages Your Angels Want You to Know by Doreen Virtue

I've been making it a regular practise to find a few minutes of quiet time and sit with a journal, connect to my guides, and let their words come through me. This will become my second book.

Here are just a few examples of the daily messages from my guides and Guardian Angels:

'Follow what lights you up. Start back up your gratitude journal. Life is magical, smell it, breathe it, taste it. Honour your soul. Celebrate. Dance. Fill your life with as much joy as you can muster. Share your joy, lift others up, and remind them of their true essence.'

'We can see how hard you are trying, and everything will stand you in good stead for the future. Believe in yourself. You were given ideas because you are capable of achieving them. There is nothing to fear. Focus only on the positive. This will bring you more of the same.'

'Be kind, be gentle, be compassionate to all living things. Everyone is struggling. See things as others see them – step outside of your awareness and feel what it must be like for them. Do not judge, just allow things to be. Raise people to where they want to be not where they are now.'

ABOUT THE SCENTED HEALING MISTS CREATED BY ANGELIC ENERGIES

When we need support and comfort in our lives, it's important to remember that the Angels are there to help us in any capacity. State of mind and emotion greatly affect our propensity to succumb to illness. To succeed in the outer world, we must first take care of our inner world. Now, more than ever, the Angels want to lift us up, fill us with courage, inner confidence, wonder and excitement. Life is suddenly full of possibility as we open ourselves up to divine guidance. What would you do if you knew you couldn't fail? The Angels can give us the courage and support to follow our dreams, to face our fears, and to move forward every day.

The series of scented healing mists have been created to help you make a connection to the Archangels and their incredible superpowers. I've always used Angel sprays while doing my energy healing to cleanse the aura and space, but I was struggling to find anything I liked on the market. Thankfully, I am blessed to have a brother who is a perfumer with Centauri Perfumes (you can see him on Fragrance View on YouTube), and with his help, and the help of the Angels (of course!), I created a beautiful range of scented healing mists using essential oils. These are all charged with Angelic Reiki and imbued with the qualities of Archangels.

Smell is incredibly powerful, transporting us back to times past; a whiff of your father's aftershave can take you straight back to childhood, for example. Aroma vibrations can by-pass the middle brain (the prefrontal cortex), the part of our mind which rationalises, analyses and censors our responses to the world, and goes straight into the memory. Aroma has an immediate effect on our soul, and we respond to it with our emotions and heart.

The scented healing mists work on many levels and come with a booklet of affirmations. Once you have given yourself a spritz, read the affirmations that go with it. The smell stays with you and keeps reminding you of the affirmations.

Each bottle is charged with Angelic Reiki, ensuring that blocked energy within our emotional, mental and spiritual bodies is dispersed, restoring the flow of life-force energy through our entire system.

These well-crafted scented healing mists are attuned to the unique strengths of different Archangels, bringing them into our lives for support and comfort in the areas we need most. They have been designed to balance and restore harmonious vibrations to cleanse our aura and the space around us, in specific alignment with the Archangels. I encourage you to use these sprays as part of your daily spiritual practise to keep you in a good place.

When you learn to consciously master the energetic realm, believe in the not yet seen, and stay in your highest frequency, you harness your innate power to create the reality you desire. That is why having a spiritual practise is vital to living a fulfilled and happy life.

We all lead such busy lives with an increasing amount of distractions vying for our attention. Without a spiritual practise, we are continually at the mercy of technology and life events pulling on our attention and emotions. Growing up we are taught to look after our body by brushing our teeth every day, eating healthily and taking exercise, but we are not taught how to look after the mind.

Carrying out a spiritual practise is like mentally going to the gym. It keeps our mind strong, grounded and focused, allowing us to connect to our own inner guidance system to help us more easily deal with challenges and stay in a healthy perspective. The scented healing mists are designed to be used as a daily spiritual practise.

DIRECTIONS FOR USE

By calling on an Archangel and their specific healing energy through the power of affirmations, you can set yourself up for a positive day full of love. To begin, close your eyes and breathe, bringing your attention to your heart, and then visualise your chest filling up with pure white light. Once you feel centred, spray the mist around the body or room, holding the intention to heal and raise vibration levels. Read an appropriate affirmation and repeat it, either aloud or in your mind's eye, while holding the intention to heal.

AFFIRMATIONS

A big part of helping you with your connection to the Archangels are the affirmations that come in the booklet that accompanies the Angelic mists. Affirmations are positive statements said in the present tense. All the power we have is in this present moment and this is a Law of Attraction universe. Whatever you put your energy into will start to manifest in your life. It is essential to understand that our unconscious mind is just like a computer, and most of us affirm unconsciously all the time. We continuously repeat thoughts until we anchor them in our mind.

If you say something consistently to yourself, e.g., 'The picture always goes wrong when I have a camera pointed at me,' then, like me, you would be hard-pressed to have a good picture taken of you. Saying, 'I'm useless with names,' guarantees that I've forgotten your name as soon as you've told me! So, words are incredibly powerful, and when they are constantly repeated until they enter the unconscious mind, they become part of our programming. A belief is just a thought that we have repeated over and over to ourselves.

When creating affirmations, it's important to understand that the unconscious mind can't compute negatives. It simply ignores them. So, for example, 'I don't want to live in this house,' translates to, 'I want to live in this house.' It would be far more effective to say, 'I am ready to move house.' It would actually be even better to say, 'I am happy & fulfilled, living in my new home,' and to visualise that statement, putting as much feeling into it as possible.

The more emotion we can put into our positive statements, the more likely they are to manifest. Feelings are emotions and emotions are energy and energy is magnetic. Affirmations are changing the energy of your mind to match what it is that you want. But what happens if our positive affirmation is so far from the existing reality that we can't connect with it emotionally? The solution is to keep feeling for a slightly better thought. Make things feel believable, as the unconscious mind is not stupid, and it knows if you are trying to trick it. But, no matter what your circumstances, there is always something to focus on that makes you feel better about the situation.

Attaining peace is quite simple in theory. It's a matter of deciding to focus on love instead of fear. It is a decision based upon your willingness to allow love into your life. Part of this decision is about changing your thoughts to be more positive. So, what are thoughts? Thoughts are just words that you tell yourself. If you catch yourself thinking a thought that is not supporting you, try saying, 'Cancel, clear and delete,' and imagine that you are re-booting your mind like a computer. This is where the art of mindfulness and meditation is so beneficial, because we realise that we are not our thoughts. We can then step outside of them and witness them, rather than allowing them to sweep us along on an emotional rollercoaster.

When we're creating our own affirmations, the most important thing is that they are written in the present tense. The quickest way to experience what you want is to affirm that you already have it. It helps you hold the vision and bring it about. Affirmations need to be repeated constantly. That's why working with the Mala beads (prayer beads) that I sell are also successful. Constantly affirm you are who you want to be, and you will soon become it.

Harnessing the power of prayer is much more effective when it is targeted at one specific being. Each healing mist is linked to a particular Archangel. The response to give help is more likely to occur if it's directed to an individual, rather than a collective. The Angels want nothing more than to be of assistance to us. We are their soul purpose, and they delight at giving us their assistance. We should never think that we can't call upon them for whatever reason. They are omnipresent beings, and therefore, they can be with more than one person in any given time or place. They do operate on a free will basis, so we have to ask for help if it is to be given.

Much the same as you wouldn't wait until your house is engulfed in flames before you called the fire brigade, don't wait until you're in total distress to call on the Angels to help. I encourage you to make it a daily practise to invite the Angels into your life. The most powerful way to give prayer is in a way that the help has already been given. This carries more energy than a desperate plea of uncertainty. That's why all the affirmations in the Angelic Energies booklet start by thanking the Archangel for their assistance. The Angels love to help, and they love to be thanked. Gratitude adds power to our prayers as it allows us to move from a place of fear to a place of appreciation. Gratitude opens our heart to receive.

As mentioned throughout the book, Einstein understood that no problem can be solved from the same level of consciousness that created it. To get ourselves out of an unwanted situation, we have to shift our mindset and align with the solution, not the problem. The easiest way to do this is to raise our vibration. Again, this is another reason why the Scented Healing Mists are so powerful. As they are charged with Angelic Reiki, they cleanse your aura and raise your vibration. By also focusing on what is wanted, rather than what is not, we are naturally elevating our consciousness.

FINAL INSIGHT FROM SOPHIE FOX AT ANGELIC ENERGIES

I have been privileged enough to attend several Angel Channelling events with the very blessed Louise Claire Webster from 'A Colourful You'. During one event she told me that I had three Archangels working with me at that moment - Archangels Raziel, Michael and Gabriel. This made complete sense to me as, at the time, I was busy writing this book. I believe Raziel was helping me understand all the spiritual knowledge that was been passed on to me, and Gabriel was helping me to communicate it. Michael is the one Angel I talk to every day without fail as I ask for his help for energetic protection. It was beautiful to get confirmation that he was listening.

Louise also gave me some very useful advice to follow, and told me about my personal Angel. She described my Angel as being ruby red and purple. Although Angels don't really have names, she was happy for me to call her Sheena. It was fascinating to learn that my Angel was with me because she's the exact opposite of me. While I have a gentle and mild-mannered nature, she is full of fire and is here to fill me with confidence and to help me fight my corner when I need to. Louise also mentioned an Angel that would be with me for the next three to four months to help bring in memories of past life experiences for a project. This Angel was described as dark purple, almost black, with the name of Mulan.

At another event, Louise told me that the Angel who will be working with me for the foreseeable future is Archangel Azrael. She was confused about this, as she knew that Archangel Azrael can be known as the Angel of death. At the time she told me this everything started to make perfect sense. This was the confirmation I needed. I had been debating whether to train in Past Life Regression and Future Life Progression with the amazing Anne Jirsch, and knowing I had Archangel Azrael's full support, I was galvanised to go ahead.

I believe I was blessed to receive guidance from Archangel Azrael to help assist the passing of one of my dearest friends recently. She and I had grown close through walking our dogs together. We'd love to be out, come rain or shine, walking all morning together. Her rapid decline following the diagnosis of cancer was a huge shock to everyone who loved her. I feel so very blessed that her beautiful family allowed me to visit her in her last few moments in this world.

I gently gave her a face and hand massage as she lay in a coma and I whispered to her the guidance I had been given to share. I assured her that she was not going to die, that she was going on to live at a higher vibration. I then explained that death was a lot like life – wherever you place your focus is what you will experience. If you don't like what you're experiencing, all you have to do is shift your perspective. With that, I gave her a kiss and told her that I was off to walk the dogs now and that I was thinking of going to the woods that she had recently showed me.

When I got home, I rounded up my dogs and we set off to the woods I had mentioned. As I was walking, I suddenly felt the presence of my friend with a wonderful uplifting energy. I could hear her voice say to me, "Well, I decided I'd had enough of lying there listening to doom and gloom and that I would much rather come for a walk with you." I laughed tears of joy and I knew in that moment she had gone. Later that afternoon, I did indeed receive confirmation that this was the case. I am so grateful to Archangel Azrael for the gentle, loving support he was able to bring through.

A big passion of mine is to offer Past Life regression and Future Life Progression via Zoom which has given incredible results. We can carry through unwanted behaviour patterns and limiting factors from previous lives, and it can be incredibly healing to have these released. Future life progression can be an invaluable tool to give you guidance as to the right decisions to make. Imagine how it would feel to have complete clarity and to be able to embody the energy of your perfect life! Experiencing this takes away any fear, doubt and confusion felt in the present moment. You are left feeling exhilarated and galvanised knowing what you are fully capable of. Future Life Progression is truly life changing!

I am also a qualified Angel Guide through Kyle Gray, and I offer Angel Guide Sessions, again via the free Zoom app. Here you will be left feeling empowered and supported by your team of spiritual helpers, while you gain valuable personal insight, wisdom and healing. You'll receive messages and guidance with the Angel cards, as well as healing and beautiful guided meditations. I talk you through how it is possible to recognise the signs and communication from your Angels to give you the confidence and awareness to be able to hear, see and feel them. Allow the Angels to transport you to a wonderful world.

If you would like to experience these sessions, or the scented healing mists, you can visit my website or catch me at many of the Mind Body Spirit Fairs around Yorkshire. Sign up on my website for the free monthly newsletter to be kept updated and inspired. If you would like to reach out to let me know how this book has helped you, please connect using the details below.

Angel Blessings X

Connect with Sophie

Website: www.AngelicEnergies.co.uk
Email: SophieFoxHealing@yahoo.com
Twitter: @AngelicNRGies
Facebook: @AngelicNRGies
Instagram: @Angelic.energies
YouTube: Angelic Energies

Subscribe to the free monthly newsletter by visiting the Angelic Energies website.

Would you like to take what you have learned here one step further and receive a clear guide on how you can enhance your life for the better?

If you've enjoyed this book and would like to fully empower yourself to become the best version of you, then the **Becoming Series** of courses are for you! Sophie has teamed up with the amazingly gifted psychic medium and energy healer Jan Costello to expand on the insights shared here. Each course guides you to become more of whom you are truly meant to be and to live in an elevated state of connection and inner peace.

The first course, "**Becoming Magical**" is designed to help you develop your intuition and enjoy a deeper connection to your Spirit Team.

- Your life will never be the same again once you have discovered how to raise your vibration and suddenly see the miracles that have been there every day.

- Life will stop feeling mundane once you learn to bring the divine into every moment.

- As your inner knowing develops, so will your confidence.

- When you learn to tap into the guidance and support that surrounds you, life will no longer feel like a battle.

- You'll have complete trust in what feels right and what doesn't which will steer you in the right direction every time.

- Everyone has the power to connect, and this course will guide you step by step in how to do so.

- To find out more, contact Sophie on the details given above.

Connect with Jan

Website: www.soulmagic.uk
Email: jan@soulmagic.uk

You are always being guided and supported. Follow what lights you up and keep in touch.

Angel Blessings,

Sophie Fox

RECEIVE DAILY INSPIRATION, COMFORT AND SUPPORT

WITH THE GUIDED BY ANGELS ORACLE CARDS

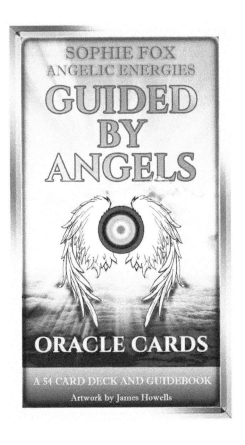

AVAILABLE AT WWW.ANGELICENERGIES.CO.UK

Guided By Angels

Lightning Source UK Ltd.
Milton Keynes UK
UKHW022257111121
393811UK00007B/193